II

GERMAN WAGE THEORIES

A HISTORY OF THEIR DEVELOPMENT

STUDIES IN HISTORY, ECONOMICS AND PUBLIC LAW

EDITED BY THE FACULTY OF POLITICAL SCIENCE OF
COLUMBIA UNIVERSITY
IN THE CITY OF NEW YORK

Volume IX] [Number 2

GERMAN WAGE THEORIES

A HISTORY OF THEIR DEVELOPMENT

BY

JAMES W. CROOK

AMS PRESS
NEW YORK

COLUMBIA UNIVERSITY
STUDIES IN THE
SOCIAL SCIENCES

24

The Series was formerly known as
Studies in History, Economics and Public Law.

Reprinted with the permission of Columbia University Press
From the edition of 1898, New York
First AMS EDITION published 1969
Manufactured in the United States of America

Library of Congress Catalogue Card Number: 72-77989

AMS PRESS, INC.
NEW YORK, N. Y. 10003

TABLE OF CONTENTS

PAGE

Introduction 7

CHAPTER I

Predecessors of Hermann 15

CHAPTER II

Hermann 23

CHAPTER III

Hermann's Successors 33

CHAPTER IV

Criticism 55

CHAPTER V

Von Thünen 68

CHAPTER VI

The Socialists 94

INTRODUCTION

Ever since political economy received its modern form at the hands of Adam Smith, the theory of wages has been in controversy. What is true of many economic questions is true of this one: the germs of later and more complete developments are found in the Wealth of Nations. Problems peculiar to the periods of historical evolution since the time of Adam Smith have brought into prominence one or more of the truths which he perceived. The system of natural liberty which he so tenaciously advocated brought the demand for its complement and condition—equality. But if the history of this century records a growing recognition of freedom for all classes, it has also disclosed an obstacle to the realization of freedom, viz., economic weakness. The demand for equality comes from the economically weak, the wage receivers. Hence, the investigation of the economic forces which determine the incomes of those classes becomes an important inquiry. Thus from a practical point of view the work done in this field by scientists of more than one nation is amply justified.

If science is not international, it ought to be so, to such an extent that the important work of one country be not unknown to another. A survey of the somewhat voluminous German literature upon the subject of wages shows that, for half a century after the publication of the Wealth of Nations, almost no original work is to be found. That there was no lack of academic activity is clear from the number of university text-books issued. These, however, for the most part repeat, summarize or but slightly modify the reasoning and conclusions of Adam

Smith. The conditions of economic life in the two countries at this period were very different. There was wanting on German soil the stimulating influence of unsolved practical problems of economics. The "industrial revolution" developed more slowly on the continent. There were lacking those conditions so favorable to the growth of industry. England's insular position allowed a degree of political unity and comparative certainty of political destiny such as was hardly possible to a continental state closely surrounded by jealous neighbors or agitated by the contending forces inherent in a loose federation.[1] The political solution must precede the economic. The English people have also possessed, to a remarkable degree, those moral capacities which underlie any considerable industrial progress, the capacity to labor and to co-operate. If we add to these facts the favorable climate, easy communication by land and sea, and abundant supplies of coal and iron, we may reasonably account for England's industrial leadership.[2]

The series of remarkable inventions, beginning with that of Hargreaves, established the factory system, stimulated the growth of industrial towns, and brought into contrast the interests of laborers and employers. While this contrast was not exactly a new one, yet it was never sufficiently intense till then to force the legal barriers to labor combination. The place which the labor problem has occupied in the British mind may be roughly measured by that legislative accumulation known as the Factory Acts, which have been a model for similar legislation by other nations.

All this is in contrast with the German condition. There the old industrial order with its restrictions and conservative methods prevailed long after England had replaced the old with the new. Schulze-Gaevernitz[3] has described the methods

[1] List, *National System*, p. 53.

[2] Hobson, *Modern Capitalism*, p. 73 ff.

[3] *Grossbetrieb*, p. 34.

which prevailed in the 18th century throughout Germany. "Everything was done by rule. Spinning came under public inspection and the yarn was collected by officials. The privilege of weaving was confined to the fraternity of the guild. Methods of production were strictly prescribed; public inspectors exercised control. Defects in weaving were visited with punishment. Moreover, the right of dealing in cotton goods was confined to the confraternity of the merchant guild; to be a master weaver had almost the significance of a public office. Besides other qualifications, there was the condition of a formal examination. The sale also was under strict supervision; for a long time a fixed price prevailed, and a maximum sale was officially prescribed for each dealer. The dealer had to dispose of his wares to the weaver, because the latter had guaranteed to him a monopoly of export trade."[1] How comparatively little progress Germany had made with machine industry under these conditions is indicated by the following facts. In 1882, 42 per cent. of the German textile industry was still conducted in the home or domestic workshop, while only 38 per cent. was carried on in factories employing more than 50 persons. More weavers were still engaged with hand looms than with power-looms, and the latter was so little developed that the hand loom could still hold its own in many articles. Knitting, lace making and other minor textile industries are still in the main home industries.[2] List, in 1844, laments the comparative infancy of German manufactures and continually seeks to impress upon his readers the industrial superiority of England. Marx finds England the paradise of capitalistic production, and although familiar with German conditions draws no important illustrations from his native country. Writing as late as 1873 he declared that political economy was in Germany a foreign science, there having

[1] Quoted by Hobson, *Modern Capitalism*, p. 78.

[2] Quoted from *Social Peace*, p. 113, by Hobson, p. 78.

existed there no soil for its growth.[1] Lassalle found German laborers unorganized and so inured to custom as to be almost deaf to his passionate appeals.

These differences between the two countries may adequately account for the great disparity in theoretic development. The existence of problems calls for solution; solution requires constructive theoretic foundations. That this is the natural order is abundantly shown in finance. Financial difficulties or problems have necessarily preceded any considerable determination of the science of finance in modern nations. The new conditions and new relations involved in machine production, or the great industry (Grossbetrieb) bring into relief the interests of classes and make necessary a scientific determination of both productive and distributive forces.

Experience has demonstrated that it is usually in connection with industries other than agricultural that the problems peculiar to the relation of employer and employed come to the front. The classes subordinated come to feel their position, they startle society by proclaiming some unusual doctrine or by performing some destructive act. Then the scientist sets about understanding the phenomena. This is the usual sequence, but the work of von Thünen would seem to furnish an exception to this order. As an agriculturalist he became impressed with the dangers involved in the existence of the economic gulf separating classes, in advance of the feelings of those classes themselves. As early as 1826 he began a series of original investigations in connection with agricultural production, which in the course of twenty five years yielded results that for originality and value may be compared with some of the best work of Ricardo. Moreover, as proof of his practical interest, and to give his theories of distribution a practical test, he used his agricultural estate for purposes of social experiment. When Rau published the first edition of his political economy (1826)

[1] Preface to 2d ed. of *Capital.*

Germany had made some start in national activity which gave rise to industrial problems. Seven years later Hermann broke the parallel course of English and German economic writing, and started Germans on a path of their own, which they have not wholly ceased to follow to this day.

Before studying theories themselves, it will be useful to take some notice of terminology. The term wages as used by the different authors does not always include the same kinds of income. It is not unnatural that men, writing under different economic conditions, and at periods so separated by time as the writers brought under review in this essay, should differ in the use of a word like wages, or a phrase like wage-class. There is great lack of unanimity even now, as will be seen by a comparison of the advocacy of different or competing views held by Walker, George or Sidgwick. As to definition, the Germans did not always follow Adam Smith. The latter said that the wages of labor were everywhere understood to be what they usually were, when the laborer was one person and the owner of the stock which employs him another.[1] This would confine wages to the income of laborers employed by owners of capital in the course of operations undertaken for a profit. It will not be necessary to point out here how Adam Smith departed from this definition in his treatment of wages.

Schmalz defines wages as the income which men receive from others for important or unimportant, honorable or despicable services. Accordingly, he classes generals, state ministers and even pensioners as wage-earners. There is nothing in his subsequent treatment to reveal the gain of such a classification.[2] Rau broadens the meaning to include what the undertaker saves out of his business to pay for his own activity—the equivalent of what he would otherwise have to pay as wages. This is the modern conception of wages of superin-

[1] *Wealth of Nations*, Rogers' ed., 1869, v. 1, p. 69.

[2] *Staatswirthschaftslehre in Briefen*, v. 1, p. 23.

tendence.[1] However, in the 8th ed. he considers that the most important case arises when over against the worker there is a wage-giver with whom he contracts for definite wages.[2] Fulda does a similar thing when he makes a part of the income of the capitalist his wages. But he has a different measure for the amount. He says the business man, during the time he is in business, must satisfy his needs for food and shelter according to the degree of his culture. He must also hold his capital in that condition which is required to prosecute his business. The part which his necessary support requires is his necessary wages; the part which his capital requires is his necessary profit.[3] Hermann restricts wages to a payment by one person to another for common services rendered. He distinguishes services as common, talented, fixed and official. For the reward of common labor he would use wages (Lohn). For the reward of labor requiring talent and education, *honorar*. The payments made by university students to professors for their lectures are at the present time called by that name. For fixed employment he uses salary (Gehalt), and for official services fee (Gage).[4] V. Thünen would also restrict wages to payment for hired labor, but he is most anxious to distinguish between the reward for labor as such, and that which is due to the tools the laborer may employ, including the simplest implements. The reward for the use of tools is interest, that for labor proper is wages.[5]

Many writers do not consider it important to state what they mean by wages, leaving the reader to infer from the general treatment the sense in which the word is used. We are,

[1] *Grundsätze der Volkswirshschaftslehre*, 4th ed., 1841, p. 201.

[2] *Ibid.*, p. 252.

[3] *Grundsätze der Oekonomisch-politischen oder Kameralwissenschaften*, 1820, 2d Ed., § 186.

[4] *Staatswirthschaftliche Untersuchungen*, 2d ed., 1870, p. 460.

[5] *Der Isolirte Staat*, Part ii, p. 78.

therefore, warned against apparent differences due to differences of terminology merely.

The plan to be pursued in this essay has occasioned some thought, and the arrangement finally adopted is not without objection. But since the chief object in making the study is to discover, if possible, progress of thought on this subject, chronology had to be sacrificed, in some instances, to a logical order. Hence while von Thünen appears after Hermann in obedience to the time order of their work, yet von Thünen appears after Brentano and Philippovich, because he is not so clearly a follower of Hermann as they are. It has often been remarked by students of the theoretical Economics of the Germans that there exists but a slender thread of logical connection between the great German writers of the last one hundred years. Indeed it has been said that the attitude toward the wages-fund theory is the only point common to most of them. But a study of the treatment by the Germans of the wages-fund, will not include the work of von Thünen, as is shown by Professor Taussig's admirable "Wages and Capital." Wishing to exhibit, if possible, the treatment of the entire wages question by the Germans, passing over rather lightly the part in each author which treats of the wages-fund, because Professor Taussig has made that familiar to English readers, and trying at the same time to give unity to my work, I have, so far as possible, grouped writers who appear to show the largest number of points of contact, and at the same time included writers of eminence who, though not connected closely with German predecessors or successors, have made important contributions to the subject. Hence all the German writers treated here are placed in two groups. One contains Schmalz, Fulda, Sartorius, Lueder, Kraus, Rau, Hermann, Brentano, Roscher, Mithoff, Mangoldt and Philippovich. Hermann is the centre of this group, and the others are important only as they lead up to him, depend upon him, deviate from him, or throw light upon him. Apart from those who come first, the common element in nearly all is the method of treatment. Other points of contact will appear as we proceed, but this is the most conspicuous. In this group there is a real unity of method and interest. The other group contains von Thünen, Karl Marx and Schulze-Gaevernitz. These authors do not belong together in the sense that the others do. They have so little in common that it is not even necessary to speak of them as a group except for convenience. They are included in this discussion because of their importance. Von Thünen was a genius, about whom it is desirable that American students should know more. A fair-minded and exhaustive study of Marx's theory of distribution, the full materials for which have but recently come into our hands, has yet to be made in English. Any earnest study of his theory of wages is welcome if it adds anything to our real understanding of Marx. Schulze-Gaevernitz is noticed here because he is the chief representative in Germany of those writers who regard wages as a residual share, and because the theory which he represents is exciting the interest of German students.

One who goes to Germany to hear lectures on the principles of Economics, or who undertakes a study of the literature of the same, must not expect to find a body of doctrines developed independently on German soil. and uninfluenced by the work of other nations. The German professor has ever on his lips the names of Adam Smith, Ricardo and John Stuart Mill. Each economist is followed, criticized or expounded according to the knowledge and idiosyncrasies of the instructor. The present German thinking has its roots in the work of the English school; and, if the German work is to be understood, the English work must be mastered first. The same thing is true of the literature. The foundations have been laid across the Channel. Hence in exposition, the theories of Adam Smith and Ricardo are often employed in this study as standards, and in this way the English and German ideas are brought into comparison.

CHAPTER I

PREDECESSORS OF HERMANN, 1776–1832

WHILE this period is the least important of all in positive results, yet a consideration of the work of a few men who wrote during this time will repay the student who desires to know the beginnings of things, and who loves to trace the development of method and theoretic spirit. When Adam Smith published the "Wealth of Nations," the physiocratic doctrines of distribution were dominant. The struggle between the views entertained by the Physiocrats and those introduced by Adam Smith was not so bitter as such struggles are apt to be. There appears to have been in Germany comparatively little objection to Adam Smith's statement. On the contrary, adherents sprang up wherever the new doctrines became known. Within a few years German students were listening to lectures delivered by University Professors who declared themselves followers of Adam Smith. However, there were some who, for various reasons, could not or would not change views already formed and expressed, and who, though partaking of the early advantages of this century, took little notice of the new movement. Among these is Schmalz,[1] whom Roscher calls the last of the Physiocrats.

[1] Theodor Anton Heinrich Schmalz was born 1760, died 1831. He studied Theology and Philosophy at the University of Göttingen, 1777–1780. He became a Professor of Law at Rinteln in 1788, but the following year was called to Königsberg, becoming Director of the University in 1801. In 1803 he was transferred to Halle as a judicial counselor and Professor, where he remained till 1808. When the new University at Berlin was established he became its first Director in 1810, and as Professor of Law continued in the service of the Prussian king.

As a writer his life was full of activity, his efforts centering principally upon

According to Schmalz, society is composed of classes or groups, differing in standard of life. Yet there is an average standard to which all groups are tending. The poor are spurred by ambition to approach the average, while shame restrains the rich from maintaining a standard far above the average. Notwithstanding the spur of ambition, wages are governed by a law. That which one is accustomed to consume in his class during the time that the work is being done determines the wages he will receive. Two reasons are assigned for this rate: 1. The laborer demands it for a life of respectability among his class. 2. It is the laborer's right. The question of right enters, because wages are obtained from men and not from nature. When a man sacrifices his time to work for me, it is right that I give him as much for it as he consumes in that time. He has also a right to receive as much for his labor as the companions of his class consume during the time in which the labor is being performed. There is no reason why he should consume more at my cost. If I give him less, I do him an injustice. If I give him more, I make him a present. Wages correspond to the amount here indicated, and that which men habitually pay by contract must have back of it the force of natural right.

It is not necessary to point out how far short of scientific precision this reasoning of Schmalz falls. Adam Smith's reasoning may leave something to be desired, but it is better than that of Schmalz. This consuming rate of Schmalz is not the same as the "lowest rate consistent with common humanity"

Politics, Law and Economics. In Politics he favored absolutism. In Law he represented the standpoint of natural right. In Economics the Physiocratics' views seemed to him the soundest. He compared the doctrines of Colbert and his followers to the Ptolemaic system of Astronomy, and those of the Physiocrats to the Copernican system, and regarded Adam Smith as a fad (see Roscher, *Geschichte*, p. 498–9). For his treatment of systematic Economics see *Handbuch der Staatswirtschaft*, Berlin, 1808, and *Staatswirtschaftslehre in Briefen*, Berlin, 1818. For his characterization by Roscher, see the latter's *Geschichte der National-Oekonomik in Deutschland*, p. 498.

of Adam Smith; the latter was a consumption rate sufficient for both the workman and his family during the entire year; the former was a rate for the workman during the time of work. Adam Smith had in mind a corrective in a decrease of the supply of labor, if the rate fell below the standard. Schmalz was appealing to conceptions of natural right.

Fulda[1] is important only as a transition from the old to the new point of view. While holding with Adam Smith that the state of wages is at once a sign and an effect of the different states of society, he attempts to show that wages may be affected by different applications of capital. To his mind machinery is inimical to the interests of labor. Wages are more favorably influenced if capital is applied to agriculture rather than to trade, since in manufacture labor is displaced by the preponderance of capital in the form of machinery. From this point of view the national interests of labor may be promoted by change of national industry and without any increase of capital.

Sartorius,[2] Lueder and Kraus were prominently instrumental in introducing the teachings of Adam Smith into Germany. In the extent to which they appeal to his views for an explanation of wages, they differ widely. Sartorius seems to have paid attention to the last page only of Adam Smith's chapter on wages, when he points out that the price of labor is regulated by (1) the demand for labor, and (2) the price of the necessaries and conveniences of life, and then follows this with a discussion of the influence of scarcity and plenty upon

[1] Friedrich Carl von Fulda, born 1774, died 1847, student at Göttingen 1794–97, and received in 1798 a call to T bingen as Professor of Kameralwissenschaft, a position which he occupied nearly forty years. His views on Economics are found in his *Grundsätse der œconomisch-politischen oder Kameralwissenschaften*, T. bingen, 1816, 2d ed., 1820.

[2] George Friedrich Sartorius was born 1766 and died 1828. After studying at Göttingen he was, in 1802, appointed by that University Professor of Philosophy, and remained in that position, although called to both Berlin and Leipsig as Professor of Kameralwissenschaft.

these two factors. Lueder [1] likewise uses only a part of Adam Smith, holding that wages will be above the minimum only when the funds from which wages are drawn increase. Kraus,[2] however, constituted himself the special interpreter of Adam Smith to the Germans; accordingly, his book read in connection with the table of contents is found to be not a word for word repetition of the "Wealth of Nations," but a good analysis of it. Thus his treatment of wages is made to include all the main points of Adam Smith.

Up to this point the German economists stated a necessary minimum wage; a new idea was originated by Lotz,[3] who first stated the conditions of maximum wages. This is the beginning of a new and more fertile treatment of the subject. Lotz pointed out that competition could operate only within certain limits, the lowest limit being subsistence wages and the upper limit that point at which wages swallow up the profits of capital. All economists since Lotz have observed some such limits. Rau was the first to elaborate the point.

Rau [4] published the first edition of his Political Economy in 1826. The doctrine of wages formulated in the first edition received scarcely any modification in the successive nine revisions, of which the last appeared in 1870. Rau was the first great German economist to recast the science on the principles laid down by Adam Smith. He may, therefore, be considered

[1] August Ferdinand Lueder, born 1760, died 1819. He was Professor of History in Braunschweig, 1797, and in 1810 Professor of Philosophy in Göttingen, where he remained till two years before his death. He published in 1800–1804, *Nationalindustrie und Staatswirthschaft.*

[2] Christian Jakob Kraus, born 1753, died 1807. He studied at Königsberg and Göttingen, and in 1780 became Professor of Practical Philosophy in Königsberg, a place which he kept till his death.

[3] Johann Friedrich Eusebius Lotz, born 1771, died 1838. He studied in Jena. He held many government appointments and was for a time Professor of Law and Economics at Bonn. He published, in 1821, *Handbuch der Staatswirthschaftslehre.*

[4] Karl Heinrich Rau, born 1792, died 1870.

the founder in Germany of that individualistic school which Adam Smith founded in England. While previous writers, who may be called followers, were for the most part mere copyists, Rau makes departures in statement and analysis. He also attempts to adapt the matter to the conditions of his own country. Rau was the first to enunciate the doctrine that wages are only a special form of price. In this he is truly a predecessor of Hermann. To understand Rau's discussion, we must recur to his doctrine of price. Price results from the combined action of three forces: (1) the value of the exchanging good, (2) the cost of the exchanging good, (3) competition. Price cannot go higher than the value cf the good to the buyer; it cannot go below the cost to the producer; it is determined somewhere between these limits by the relation of supply and demand. Turning now to his discussion of wages, the value of labor is regulated by the purposes for which it is applied. In most cases it is applied to secure a profit. When so employed, the undertaker is in a position to give high or low wages according to the amount of net product left over after other expenses are paid. It might go so high as to swallow up the pure profit of the undertaker, and even so high as to decrease interest and rent, but it cannot destroy them, because in that case undertaking must cease. But from the fact that even pure profit usually exists, it is evident that we need other determining principles.

We take a further step in advance by applying the principle of costs to labor, which, in skilled occupations, includes subsistence and previous outlay for training; while in simple occupations, subsistence, broadly interpreted to include family support during the intervals of idleness, is the principal consideration. Costs are determined by (1) the usual manner of life of the laborer and his family in given conditions of climate, customs, and the degree of culture of the people as a whole, as well as that of the peculiar class to which the laborer may happen to belong; (2) the price of the commodities which enter into the laborer's consumption list. In this way is determined the cost of production of labor. Wages cannot remain permanently below this cost, for in that case the supply of labor would fail. Here we have the limit to the fall of wages. The limit to the rise of wages has already been given. Between the limits there is a wide margin. The force that determines whether wages shall tend to the maximum or to the minimum, or remain intermediate, is competition: the competition of labor for capital and the competition of capital for labor. The supply of labor consists in the number of men who are resolved to work for wages and are seeking work. The demand for labor consists in the amount of capital which is destined to be applied to the employment of laborers in profitable undertaking. If the population is very large in comparison with the amount of capital, then wages may sink to the minimum or below it before correction comes. In the opposite case, it may rise till reduced profits correct the tendency.

In these views Rau differed but slightly from the English school as known in his time. Adam Smith and Ricardo both conceived a hypothetical price which they called natural, *above and below* which actual market price might fluctuate. Rau designated an upper and lower limit *between* which actual price might fluctuate. Rau's lower limit is really identical with Ricardo's central point. The fluctuations in both cases are caused by the same influence, *i. e.*, relation of supply and demand. In designating the upper limit, as the value of the good to the buyer, the first step was taken toward regarding the influence of the consumer on price, which in the hands of Hermann developed into a theory designed to refute the wages-fund doctrine. There is one other respect in which Rau and the English school differ: as to the part of the theory upon which special emphasis shall be laid. After Ricardo makes the distinction between natural and market wages, he says almost nothing further about market wages. He seems to have developed his system of distribution from the point of view of his conception of natural wages. If so, he would naturally lay greater emphasis upon it, as his readers would thereby the better understand him. In the passages in which he repudiates supply and demand as determinants of prices, he is to be understood not as denying their influence on market price, but as denying their power to determine natural price, in which he is chiefly interested. It was not so with Rau Ricardo's determinant of natural wages became for him one of the limits of fluctuation and the determinants of the fluctuations assumed the central place. We might therefore expect from Rau a more careful study and statement of the principles of supply and demand in their application to the problem of wages. To say that wages depend upon the relation of supply and demand is to say almost nothing at all. We want something more than a definition of the terms employed in one short sentence. Such expressions as that, when capital is large in comparison with population wages rise, and when population is large in comparison with capital wages fall, are too indefinite, and bring in direct comparison things which strictly are incapable of comparison.

The foregoing discussion shows that Rau is far superior to his German predecessors. But, in justice to them, it must not be forgotten that he wrote under the influence not only of Adam Smith, but of Malthus, McCulloch, Torrens, Ricardo, and James Mill. This is proved by the fact that in the first edition of his work on political economy, he makes frequent reference to these authors whose works had been translated into German or French. It is also proved by the fact that many of his general propositions are found in the English works. For instance, his remarks on the proportions between capital and labor as determining wages are found in substantially the same form in James Mill.

Any lack of economic analysis tending to mar the work of the early German economists is fully atoned for by the publication in 1832 of Hermann's "Economic Investigations." This work marks a great advance on previous theoretical economic studies, and even to-day exercises considerable influence on economic thought.

CHAPTER II

HERMANN[1]

HISTORICALLY considered, the "Economic Investigations" of Hermann possesses a unique interest. Unlike Adam Smith, whose "Wealth of Nations" appeared at the end of a long career, Hermann began his extended activity in economic literature with the publication of the work by which he is chiefly known, and which won from Roscher the judgment that it placed its author "among the most eminent economists of the nineteenth century."

To the reviewer of the progress of economic theory in Germany, the work marks an important advance. Finance and Administration were ably and independently treated previous to 1832. But of the many names which appear among contributors on pure Economics during the half century following the publication of the "Wealth of Nations," Rau is really the only one of note, and in power of analysis and independent thought he is much inferior to Hermann. That the work of the former was always more familiar to ordinary students must be admitted; but that is due to the fact that Hermann's style is more difficult, while Rau's book has decided pedagogical advantages.

It is to Hermann's credit that, living in a country which was then far behind England in commercial and industrial development, and hence behind her in the development of capitalistic production, and the advanced relations of laborer and employer, he should have been the first to assail, with some

[1] Freidrich Benedikt Wilhelm v. Hermann, born 1795, died 1868.

measure of success, the wages-fund theory of the English economists, and substitute for it a theory which appears in nearly every systematic treatise on political economy in Germany since his day.

I.

In the early German wage literature there appears little to which Hermann is indebted. The numerous writers previous to Rau are either avowedly expositors of Adam Smith or mere copyists. He, however, owes something to Rau. Rau was the first German economist to treat wages as only a special form of price and to apply the general principles already evolved under his treatment of price to a solution of the problem of wages.

It is from this point of view that Hermann opens his discussion of wages. According to both men, the general principle is supply and demand, but to Hermann this, so stated, means but little. We need to trace back the causal connection one step further. Taking the demand side first, there are three factors which determine price.[1] First, the individual value of the good to the buyer. Secondly, the buyer's ability to pay for the good. Thirdly, the disposition to buy as cheaply as possible; the buyer will therefore pay no more than the price reduced by the competition of the sellers. Turning now to the supply side of the problem. There are here, too, three factors. First, the seller must receive as much as the good has cost. Secondly, the disposition to get as much as possible; the seller will therefore get as much above cost as the buyers raise the price. Thirdly, much depends upon the exchange value of the means of exchange. If in the above principles we will substitute for seller, buyer and good, the words laborer, employer and labor, we shall have in outline the principles according to which wages are determined.[2]

[1] *Staatswirthschaftliche Untersuchungen*, 1870, p. 390–459.

[2] *Staatswirthschaftliche Untersuchungen*, p. 460–487.

Unfortunately, Hermann never finished the discussion, having treated the subject from the standpoint of demand only. How he would have considered the problem of population under the cost of production of laborers we have no means of knowing. Although the treatment as we have it is defective, yet we may adopt a point of view according to which the apparently one-sided treatment may yield results. If we note that population does not readily respond to fluctuations in demand for laborers, we may assume the supply side of the problem as a fixed quantity. Then a correct statement of the principles of demand may yield the determinant of wages for short periods; *i. e.*, assuming Hermann's method to be a correct one.

Hermann's views may be conveniently considered under five heads.

I. The first important question is, to whom, or to what class is labor valuable? who are the real buyers of labor? To these questions Adam Smith, Ricardo and James Mill had given the unequivocal answer, the employer of labor—the capitalist. But Hermann answered that the real consumer of labor power, and hence the class to which it has value, is the class which consumes the laborers' products. The nature of the case is not changed by the fact that the producer hires and rewards the labor directly, while the consumer is unconscious of the labor involved in the product. The consumer is nevertheless a buyer of labor. The undertaker is considered by Hermann a mere labor purveyor, a sort of consumers' agent, who for his outlay in wages seeks a recompense in the price of the goods made by labor.

This doctrine, not elaborated, but rather treated as self-evident, is the foundation-stone of Hermann's theoretic structure, and upon its truth or falsity will depend the soundness or weakness of his alleged contribution to this subject.

II. While Menger properly has the credit of working out in detail, and tracing to some important result the conception of stages in the productive process, the idea is clearly suggested by Hermann. Only a small fraction of the number of laborers engaged in productive activities are employed in putting on the finishing touches to commodities. Many are getting out the raw materials, and between miners and agriculturalists at one end of the line, and labourers ministering directly to consumers' needs at the other, there are whole groups of laborers pushing along the commodities from a lower to a higher stage in the transformations from crude products of nature to the manifold refined forms suited to serve man's wants.

Hermann makes use of the theory to establish a point which seems not to have attracted the attention of subsequent writers. Most theorists since Adam Smith have felt the necessity of distinguishing between particular and general wages. They considered that when they had determined a general law of wages they had not accounted for differences of wages in different employments. Hence we have repeated so often both in English and German treatises Adam Smith's familiar points: wages in particular employments are determined by differences in agreeableness of employment, expense of learning, trust reposed, etc. Hermann offers a different view when he proclaims a difference in wages according as the employment is remote from, or adjacent to, the final stage. Bakers and butchers always receive higher wages than weavers, and those are in the most unfavorable position who are laboring in the initial stages of production, as in mining and agriculture. The explanation of these alleged facts is that the final products are subject to constant daily demand, and the dealer in such commodities can and must offer his laborers higher wages than he who produces what can remain for a considerable time in one stage. The dealer in the intermediate products must make good his wage outlay in the price of the product, and in order to insure this he keeps wages at as moderate a figure as possible. All who purchase from him buy as cheaply as possible. This means that a constant pressure is brought to bear on all those in the previous labor steps to limit the wage outlay. "Upon all the production stages there rules the economic motive to furnish to the final purchaser as cheaply as possible the labor contained in the product." The producer of the final product is not so pushed, since his commodity is subject to pressing daily demand.

In connection with this there is a subordinate point which is worth mentioning. What are the general principles according to which a change of price of goods in the final stage will affect wages in the earlier stages? Hermann answers that this depends upon the time during which the product delays at a given stage. The shorter the time, the more sensitively will the rate of wages respond to changes in the stages above. It will also depend upon the readiness with which undertakers and laborers can betake themselves to other employments. Something depends also upon whether the raw material or the partly-manufactured product is limited to a definite use, or is capable of several applications.

III. Mere demand or desire is powerless to affect wages unless there exists also the ability to pay. To know this, one must know the source of payment. Adam Smith and his immediate followers considered income and capital as the true sources of all payments for wages. Ricardo laid emphasis upon capital alone. Against Ricardo's view Hermann took a decided stand. A mere statement of his argument reveals strong feeling. Whoever would get the labor he needs or wants must have the means to pay. In the case of household servants it is plain that they are paid from income. With the fluctuation of incomes, fluctuates the effective demand for servants. It is evident that to pay them out of the stock of accumulated wealth would be wastefulness.

There is no labor which does not pertain to a last consumer. This is as true of labor, for labor contractors or undertakers, as of labor in direct personal service. However numerous the technical steps in the production may be, the finished product at last becomes an object of use, either temporary or lasting. All the intervening steps from the beginning to the end have been taken for the sake of this ultimate use. And the final recompense for all previous outlays must find its source in the payments for the use of these final objects. "Not merely all the labor applied to every labor step in producing the immediate product, but also the labor contained in the replacing and use of all kinds of fixed capital, is at last to be made good by the payments which the ultimate consumer of the product makes."[1] The wage outlay of the last, as well as of all previous steps of manufacture, is contained in the price of the final product. Capital cannot be the source of wage payment, for if restitution out of the product fails, production and hence wage-payment must cease. If production were continued without reference to the final demand, the depreciation in value of the raw products would be a severe experimental demonstration to the producer that his capital was not the source of wage payment. Hence we get the following result. The true and continuous source of the compensation of production is the income of the buyer of products for his own use. Capital is only the help-means to production, not the source of reward. "It is unthinkable that wages depend upon the greatness of the disposable capital in relation to the number of laborers."[2] It depends in the long run always upon the price which the active buyers can and are willing to pay for the product. "To hold that the source of wages is capital is not merely a theoretical error, but also in practical affairs is a doctrine of the most serious importance; because it fortifies the laborer in the superficial view that the undertaker is his wage-giver, and that upon him depends the scale of his wages. If the laborer holds to such an appearance of the truth and becomes hostile to the undertaker, participating in acts of violence against him, there is no cause for surprise. That the doctrine of science should

[1] *Staats. Unters.*, p. 473. [2] *Ibid.*, p. 477.

strengthen the selfish procedure of ignorant laborers in strikes, by its doctrine that the source of wages is the capital of the 'entrepreneur,' shows the need for caution."[1]

IV. The two considerations, need of labor service and ability to pay, are operative from the side of the "entrepreneur." But these are conditions which relate to but one of the contractors. It is obvious that in general under the régime of free competition, whoever employs labor will not grant higher pay than the lowest at which he can obtain the appropriate service in sufficient quantity. How low wages may go is influenced somewhat by the competition of laborers. Unfortunately Hermann did not profess to have treated the wage question from the side of supply in any thorough manner. We do not find that he took account of numbers and the forces which determine them. He confined himself to a few remarks on forces which prevent the ready access of labor to the market. Long before Cairnes[2] wrote on non-competing groups, Hermann had said that efficient competition in the labor market exists only between groups with approximately like technical skill. A man's power to compete is limited to the employments with which he has some familiarity. For an entire group, the duration of this limitation is the time which the young generation requires to fit itself for a new occupation, *i. e.*, an occupation differing from the one usual to the group.

But the hindrances are not confined to those between groups; even within the group there are barriers in the cost of travel; delays in changing settlement; reluctance to receive strangers; difference in speech and custom; the lack of sociability, and religious prejudice, etc., etc.

V. So much for direct competition. But Hermann regards indirect competition as often more real and effective than direct. This is the labor involved in competing goods. "It shows

[1] *Staats. Unters.*, p. 478.

[2] *Some Leading Principles of Pol. Econ.*, p. 66.

itself in the quantity of foreign products sold, which necessarily withdraws from our laborers just so much opportunity for labor as the foreign importations would have required on our part, had we made the goods." This withdrawal of opportunity to labor arises as soon as the foreign product can be sold somewhat cheaper than that produced with home labor."[1] If the home production is to continue, either wages must be lowered, or other changes in the conditions of production must be made. Hermann was well aware of the importance of the factors of production other than labor. Equal labor with him does not always mean equal efficiency. He adduces many examples to show that the products of higher paid labor can hold the market against products of cheaper paid labor. When Hermann wrote, wages were higher in England than in Germany, yet cotton and iron were regularly imported into the latter country. The result was that the higher paid English labor displaced the cheaper paid German labor. He laid down the general proposition that those laborers can command the market whose products can on the whole be sold cheaper.[2] It was clear to him that many elements besides wages must be taken into account in commanding a market. Cost of raw material, access to sources of power, facilities of transportation, efficient management and efficient labor are all of importance. When all these elements are given proper weight, it is clear that it is possible for a country to command a market, and at the same time to pay high wages. It is equally true, however, that by inattention to conditions of production other than labor conditions, or by relative disadvantage with reference to these conditions, a body of laborers may be entirely defeated in their endeavors to raise wages by limitation of their numbers through lower birth rate. If the limited home supply of labor diminished the home product, there is no guarantee that prices will rise, since foreign competition may prevent it.[3]

[1] *Staatsw. Unters.*, p. 483. [2] *Ibid.*, p. 483. [3] *Ibid.*, p. 483.

II

Hermann's treatment of indirect competition, at first sight, seems to lend support to the chief contention of the protectionist in respect to wages. The free trade doctrine has enjoyed no slight advantage, in that it could quote in its support the teachings of nearly all the respectable economists for a century or more. It would be no slight gain if the authority of Hermann could truthfully be used in support of protection. While some support might be gained from him, it will appear from the statement given above that he was free from some of the commonest errors observed in the modern discussions of the tariff. It would be hard to find in his discussion support for the "pauper argument," unconnected, as it commonly is, with rigid investigations as to conditions of production other than labor conditions. It is too often assumed that "cheap" labor will inevitably displace more highly paid labor. According to Hermann's view, pauper labor, far from being a dangerous competitor of better paid labor, might easily be displaced by the latter. The real importance of indirect competition, then, lay in the fact that such competition was made possible by various favorable conditions of production. By this means capital might be the laborer's most relentless competitor, thus rendering useless his efforts to better his condition by limiting his numbers.

The treatment of direct competition is open, of course, to the charge of inadequacy, but this is true of all beginnings. It is less to Hermann's discredit that he did not complete the theory, than it is to his followers, that they ignored the theory altogether. The objections which have been urged against Cairnes' idea of the limits of competition in group arrangement may be urged against Hermann's idea. They may both have truly described conditions at the time, but the extension of machinery and modern methods of production makes modification necessary. Both writers appear to have had in mind principally a sort of contingent, not an actual, competition. It depended upon the transference of the young from the occupation of parents to other kinds of work. The theory was intended to answer the question, What is the force of a man's competition if he tries to change his occupation? It did not determine actual competition should a man remain in his occupation.[1] On Hermann's part the doctrine was negative. This is due to the fact that he did not complete the study as we may suppose he had planned.

His idea that wages are high or low according as the labor is near to, or remote from, the final stage of production, is new and interesting, but does not seem to have large support from facts. By comparing wages paid in the earlier stages of production with those in the later, facts could be found which would seem to support a directly opposite conclusion. He points out no limited special talent as necessary to perform the labor near the final stage. He notices no obstacles to competition in the final group which do not apply to other groups. He provides for competition in all the groups from the new populations, and it does not appear clear why in a few generations migrations from other groups would not reduce wages to a general level for like skill. If there were reasons in general economic conditions why the highest wages could be paid for work on the final stage, and it were actually offered, there would be a tendency to overcrowd those occupations, a tendency which would result in reducing wages to the level of pay in other occupations.

The most interesting point, and certainly the most important for later developments of wage theories in Germany, is Hermann's treatment of the wages-fund theory. But this point is so intimately connected with the teachings of Hermann's successors that a discussion of it will be deferred till the group to which Hermann belongs is brought under review.

[1] J. B. Clark, *Limits of Competition*. See Clark and Giddings, *Modern Distributive Process*.

CHAPTER III

HERMANN'S SUCCESSORS

THERE are a number of economists who are the followers of Hermann in the sense that they are influenced by his teachings, but Brentano is one in the sense that he made additions to Hermann's theory. Although Brentano has made several contributions to the subject in recent years, nothing more fundamental has appeared on his theory of wages since he published the essay in Hildebrand's Jahrbücher, in 1871, on "Die Lehre von den Lohnsteigerungen mit besonderer Rücksicht auf die englischen Wirthschaftslehrer."[1] This is a criticism of the English views on wages, in the course of which his own ideas are made apparent. The central point of his criticism is his opposition to the fixity of the fund involved in the doctrine of the wages-fund, as taught by the leading economic writers up to that time. He exonerates Adam Smith from the imputation of having conceived the fund as a fixed quantity; for, although he was the first to use the word, fund, and to speak of it as a source of wages, when capital and land are introduced as claimants of a share in the production, wages no longer correspond with total production, and from this point on, are not conceived as fixed by the amount of a fund. Having placed Adam Smith to one side as not open to criticism on this point, Brentano proceeds briefly to show that when other economists thought they were basing their doctrine on a fixed fund, they were mistaken. Ricardo's doctrine of the relation between wages and profit assumes a fixed amount. At the same time his theory of the standard of life

[1] See *Jahrbücher für Nationaloekonomie*, I Folge, vol. xvi, pp. 251–281.

as determining wages makes fixity impossible, depending as a standard does upon the laborers' subjective measure of life-needs. This charge, however, of a lack of consistency between two parts of a theory does not seem to be well founded, from the fact that so far as Ricardo considered the standard of life as determining wages, it was a minimum standard which he had in mind, and this he conceived as constant for long periods. Brentano also denies Senior's claim to have established the fixity of the fund upon a scientific basis. According to Senior, the wages-fund depends upon the relation in which the entire product is distributed between laborers and capitalists on the margin of cultivation. This relation depends upon the rate of profit, which in turn depends upon the surplus above the cost of labor. In short, the fund which determines wages is itself determined by wages. John Stuart Mill is as little successful as the others in establishing the fixity of the fund. Having placed certain limitations upon the terms employed, Mill holds that wages depend upon the relation of population and capital. He further states that they cannot be affected by anything else. "Wages cannot rise, but by an increase of the aggregate funds employed in hiring laborers, or by a diminution in the number of competitors for hire; nor fall, except either by a diminution of the funds devoted to paying labor, or by an increase in the number of laborers to be paid."[1] He here assumes a certain degree of fixity, but Brentano points out that Mill's idea of capital allows very little definiteness to the fund, since he made the distinction between capital and not-capital to centre wholly in the intention of the owner. Human intention as to the particular employment of wealth is too changeable to allow fixity to be predicated of its object. For instance, the ordinary exigencies of life may require that what to-day was intended to be devoted to the employment of labor may to-morrow be spent on a journey. An

[1] *Principles of Political Economy*, Book ii, ch. xi, § 1.

increased demand for goods might easily change the wages-fund by a change in the mind of the capitalist as to the destination of wealth in his possession.

Thornton discussed at considerable length the possibility of an increase of wages, either at the cost of consumers by compelling them to pay higher prices for commodities, or at the cost of employers through a diminution of profits. He argued that it could be at the cost of consumers only if there arose a relative increase of demand for consumable goods, or a relative decrease of product by monopoly. According to Thornton's view, in whatever way consumers are forced to bear the burden of the higher wage in one branch, it will be found that their power of demand for other commodities has been proportionately weakened, and thus laborers in other branches suffer a corresponding loss. It is evident that, if we entertain Thornton's view, although we may not hold to a fixed wages-fund, we really substitute for the latter a fixed income-fund, and must admit the truth of the opinion held by the wages-fund theorists that one class of laborers can increase their wages only at the expense of another class. Brentano holds that Thornton has here made a mistake, which consists in not sufficiently analyzing the changed economic conditions of laborers as consumers, brought about by a rise in their wages. By assuming a fixed income, it is true that by so much as income is allowed to expand in one direction it must contract in another. But Brentano continues to argue that by the very conditions of the supposition, the laborers' income is not fixed, but increased. Therefor, in their case no contraction is necessary. Furthermore, the extra demand upon the incomes of others by increase of price is exactly counterbalanced by an increased wage or purchasing power on the part of laborers. Hence an increase of wages, by the method supposed, is not a detriment to other laborers, nor is it inimical to national accumulation, if secured at the expense of employers, for by as much as capitalists have less inducement, laborers have greater power to save.

So far the work of Brentano seems to be purely negative, but taken in connection with his position in regard to the source of wages, both ultimate and proximate, it is enough to show the trend of his thinking. His ideas as to the source of wages is made clear in the article in the Jahrbücher, and in some of his later works.[1] The capitalist secures control of laborers' products by supporting laborers out of his capital. In whatever form it may come, there is the purpose and expectation that the value will all return to the capitalist out of the income of the consumers of his product. Since what consumers offer is no settled amount, the wages-fund theory overlooked the "possibility of rolling off upon consumers the higher wages demanded by coalitions; it overlooks the fact that an employer will always be ready to expend more capital in the payment of wages as soon as the consumers replace for him the sum expended thereon, and that in such a case it will always be possible for him, if he himself has no more than a certain capital, to procure capital by borrowing abroad."[2]

We see how closely he follows Hermann in admitting the entrepreneur's possessions as the immediate source of wages, but denying that they perform the important function assigned by the wages-fund theorists. The capital of the employer is the source of wages in the first instance, but the employer himself is only a link in the chain, and that a very dependent one; for consumers control the situation. If the latter show willingness to consume at remunerative prices, capital can expand to an unlimited amount by anticipation under our credit system. This view necessitates the surrender of the idea of a fixed wage fund. The effective criticism of that postulate of English political economy is the important contribution of Brentano to this subject, based as the criticism is upon Hermann's positive contributions. Hermann's criticism consists largely in an interpretation of economic organization, as related

[1] See *Relation of Labor to Law*, p. 214. [2] See below. p. 37.

to the laboring man, which made necessary a different view of the nature of the "fund" from that of the English school. Brentano was not content with this, but pursued the enemy into his own camp. He showed that, as judged by the very writings of those who championed the doctrine most strongly, it must suffer discredit.

From his criticism of Ricardo and Mill, as of others, it is clear that Brentano does not believe in the fixity of the wages-fund. But his account of the manner in which the capital in employers' hands, which he regards as the immediate source of wages, can be changed in amount, shows that there are definite limits to the fluctuation of capital. One common method was shown by Brentano in his criticism of Mill. An employer might change his mind. But while this might affect to some extent the fixity of the funds of an individual capitalist, it becomes of less importance when applied to capitalists as a class, for an average change of intentions by a large number of employers might result in something approaching a constant. The same remark holds for the other cause—the use of credit. If an individual capitalist is in mind, there may be some truth in the possibility of increasing wage-paying power by credit, but when applied to all capitalists the use of credit for such purposes has definite limits.

In general, we may say that Brentano's criticism of the English economists makes clear his view that the source of wages is elastic, and that his treatment of Thornton's opinions shows that Brentano regarded as possible an advance of wages to workers in one branch of industry, without necessity of loss to workers in other branches. Yet the whole treatment fails clearly to distinguish between the operations of individual capitalists and the operations of capitalists as a body.

Roscher's contribution is rather insignificant. As usual with the Germans, he opens the discussion by assigning to supply and demand the highest importance. Each element is considered by itself in the discussion. The supply of labor is determined by the prevailing standard of life. And since the standard is determined by laborers, therefore the supply of labor is determined by laborers. Thus one important factor of those which determine wages is under the control of wage-receivers. Roscher seems to have understood the real significance of this fact without assigning too much importance to it. It is not true, of course, that present laborers have control of present supply. To say that laborers have control of labor-supply can only mean that present laborers can control future supply. How important this may be as a basis for shifting upon laborers the responsibility for their own condition, depends upon how thoroughly we hold to the solidarity of labor as a sort of corporate responsibility by which the present generation is held responsible for the doings of the past generation. Responsibility is of two kinds, natural and moral. Natural responsibility for past errors, either of themselves or of their ancestors, laborers cannot escape. The sins of the fathers are visited upon the children. But the moral responsibility for the errors of a former time cannot be ascribed to the present. But the case may be different in respect to the accountability of the present for the future. It is certain that, physically speaking, the supply of the laboring population twenty years hence will depend upon the action of population for the next ten years. But there is nothing in the nature of things that could indicate what laboring population is necessary twenty years hence. So that present increase is based upon present conditions, and the future must take care of itself; just as past conditions determined past increase, and the present must deal as best it can with numbers such as they are. Although Roscher does not enter at all upon this line of reasoning, he sees enough to admit that labor's control over its own supply has this limitation: that the laboring class as a body can benefit by it only after long periods of time, and that for the moment the control is of slight advantage, because the whole present supply must be carried to market for support.

Demand, according to Roscher, depends upon the value in use of labor and purchasers' capacity to pay. While the standard of life fixes minimum wages, value in use determines maximum wages. Under value in use he merely approves v. Thünen's point that additional product in any branch of industry, due to the labor of the last workman employed, has a controlling influence on the rate of wages. He connects capacity to pay in a vague way with national income. In this it is easy to trace the influence of Hermann. But the points, when not fragmentary, are confused. Hermann is also followed in the opinion that the capital of the employer is not the source of wages, but acts as a sort of reservoir for the payment of wages. Demand for labor does not depend upon the size of the national capital. This view is supported by calling attention to the effect of the different uses of capital upon the demand for labor. "Every transformation of circulating into fixed capital diminishes the demand for other labor." "Only that part of circulating capital can affect wages which is intended, directly or indirectly, for the purchase of labor."[1] He likewise follows Hermann in the view that the highest wages are paid to those who are employed on the last stages of the productive processes.

This is enough to show how little of originality is to be found in this part of Roscher's work. At the same time it is enough to indicate his proper historical place on the question of wages. The method is that of Rau and Hermann, while the ideas are mostly those of the latter. While the treatment is much weaker than that of the one from whom he chiefly draws his material, the inclusion of von Thünen's undeveloped doctrine of the influence of marginal laborers on wages, having no organic connection with other parts of Roscher's work, implies, in addition, a careless attitude of mind on the whole question.

Mithoff[2] seems to have adopted Roscher's treatment as an

[1] Roscher, *Pol. Econ.*, v. 2, p. 55.

[2] See Schönberg's *Handbuch der Politischen Oekonomie.*

outline for his own discussion. The standard of life, the elements of which he states in detail, here also determines minimum wages and is treated under supply, while the usefulness of labor and money demand (Zahlungsfähigkeit) determine maximum wages. The larger part of his treatment comes under ability to pay, and is hence an attempt to give a more precise determination to the wages-fund. It must be confessed that the exposition is somewhat hackneyed. The capital of the employer and that of others over which he has control by means of credit is a reservoir for the payment of wages. What flows out of the reservoir in the form of wages is restored by consumers of the goods produced by labor's help. Hence consumers are the buyers of labor, and their income, or that portion which is paid to labor, is the true source of wages. This is, however, not a fixed amount in the sense that it remains fixed during a productive period as it was at the beginning. At any moment it is a fixed, but not a foreordained amount. If at any moment we divide this amount by the number of laborers, the quotient is the average wage. However, Mithoff shows his practical turn of mind and his agreement with Brentano by asking what purpose such a procedure would answer. The amount of capital, however, applied to the purchase of labor is unknown. If it is a certain sum to-day, by a change of rate it is a different sum to-morrow. A change of rate is possible by a transference of part of the profits to wages, or by drawing more heavily upon consumers. "If neither of these assumptions can be made, then the undertakers will not apply a greater amount of capital to the purchase of labor. In this case, certainly, the average rate of wages remains dependent upon the capital which the undertakers determine shall be applied to the purchase of labor." However, the amount is not made unchangeable during the production period. How much of the national income is applied to payment of wages depends upon two factors: the first is direction of consumption; the second is the character of productive industries. "If consumption seeks preponderatingly for such goods as require for their production much human labor, a greater part of the national income is required for the purchase of labor than would be required if such goods were consumed which required less labor and more capital and a larger draught upon nature's powers." If we suppose an increase of total capital the evolution of technical branches of production will promote a more universal application of capital and a diminished use of human labor.

We perceive that Mithoff's views are for the most part such as we find in the works of his predecessors. We have supply and demand as the great law, supply as connected with cost of labor, demand for labor as connected with its utility, and lastly consumers' income as the true source of wages, which is but a repetition of Hermann's view. How much consumers contribute to wages depends, he says, upon the direction of consumption and the character of productive industries. If consumption takes the direction of demanding goods chiefly made by labor, wages tend upward; or, if the state of the arts is such that what is demanded is made largely by machinery, human labor is displaced and wages tend downward. The comments of Professor Taussig[1] on this point are so admirable that I shall be pardoned for quoting him. After pointing out that this reasoning as to the direction of consumption is derived apparently from Roscher, who states that the demand for unskilled labor is much affected by the direction which consumption takes, being greater if the luxury of the rich takes the form of hiring many dependents, and less if expenditure takes modern form, he continues: * * * "The whole consideration of the direction of consumption as affecting wages, the discussion of demand for hand-made goods or machine-made goods * * all goes back to consumers' demand or income as the source of wages. It can really bear, therefore, only on the

[1] *Quarterly Journal of Economics*, v. 9, p. 10.

demand for one sort of labor as compared with another. * * * The form which it takes with Mithoff, and apparently with Roscher, overlooks the simple fact that machines are made by labor, and that a demand for machine-made goods affects, not the total demand for labor, but the direction of demand (say) towards laborers who make and tend shoe machinery rather than towards old-fashioned cobblers."

There is a good deal in Mangoldt to remind one of Senior, both in spirit and in treatment of the subject. Senior, however, did not employ such terminology as to obscure rather than illuminate his text, nor did he cumber the treatment with such barren analysis. Mangoldt's teachings agree for the most part with contemporary English political economy. This is seen most clearly, perhaps, in his treatment of the wages-fund. The supply of the means of support of labor is said to constitute the demand for labor. This supply makes up the greater part of circulating capital. For theoretical purposes, says Mangoldt, we may treat circulating capital and means of support of labor as identical, and say that wages are determined by the relation of circulating capital to labor supply. But this comes dangerously near saying that wages are determined by the relation of labor supply to wages. This declaration so lacks in scientific precision that it may not be improper for Professor Taussig to say that Mangoldt "gives the subject a wide berth." His fragmentary treatment may be exemplified by the fact that, like Roscher, he merely approves one of von Thünen's most important points, but makes no use of it in further discussion. He says the demand for labor proceeds from employers, and can continue only so long as the service of labor surpasses in value that which the employer pays in the form of wages. Since employers apply labor to the most productive parts of their business, and only have recourse to less productive parts as more labor is employed, it is possible to say that the wages which secures equilibrium between supply and demand is of like importance with the anticipated pure return of the labor last applied.[1]

The treatment of our subject by Philippovich[2] is of interest because he endeavors to give a systematic account of Political Economy as it now stands. He does not represent any economic school, but tries to retain the best from all writers, and thus exhibit a progressive science. His method is thoroughly German, following as he does Rau and Hermann in treating wages as only a part subject, under price of commodities. If faithfully followed, this method insures the inclusion in the discussion of all the important commercial influences upon wages. To avoid error, however, it is necessary to notice in what respects labor differs from commodities. Philippovich escapes this error only in part. He merely mentions the laborer's relations to the thing which the laborer sells. Since the laborer cannot separate himself from his labor-power, and the fulfilling of the labor contract involves the use of the man, the wage-question involves more or less the physical, moral, spiritual and social welfare of wage-earners. These non-material elements of the problem affect the practical working out of the forces of supply and demand. In critical periods of the relation of employers and employed, the local bonds of workmen preventing movement, as well as lack of accumulated means of support, operate against them. The ease with which employers organize, and their command of the supplies of life, give them the advantage in the struggle, and as a consequence laborers are apt to suffer in their rate of wages.

These are obvious considerations, and were well expressed long ago by Adam Smith. The peculiar bearing which they ought to have upon the method employed by nearly all the economists of the group now under consideration, will be noticed when we have finished the exposition of Philippovich's

[1] *Grundriss der Volkwirthschaftslehre*, p. 158.

[2] *Grundriss der Politischen Oekonomie.*

views. Philippovich follows Hermann in the manner in which he examines the forces of supply and demand. On the side of demand we have (1) the number of undertakers; (2) the amount of service desired by them; (3) their valuation of the service; (4) their ability to pay. On the side of supply we have (5) the number of those desiring work; (6) amount of service demanded of workers; (7) laborers' own valuation of labor power; (8) value of money paid for labor.

I. The influence of the number of employers, says our author, lies in competition. The more employers there are, the more will wages have a tendency to rise. From this point of view it would seem that laborers' interests are inimical to the concentration of industry. If this be true, laborers have a discouraging prospect ahead. But our author does not hint that laborers have any control in the matter. Whether a country shall have a large or small number of employers depends upon many conditions, he says, among which are the degree of culture, distribution of wealth, the organization of credit, and the manifoldness of the directions of production. None of these is under the control of laborers.

II. The amount of labor which is sought for in the general labor market is determined by the amount of land and capital which the owners employ in productive industry. The strength of this labor demand is much affected by the distribution of wealth and the productivity of wealth. Individuals who own large amounts of wealth apply a larger proportion to direct satisfactions than those who have small possessions, since the latter are more strongly moved to the increase of income. Concentration of wealth, then, in the hands of single individuals is a hindrance to the demand for labor. If wealth has become less productive, there may be increased activity in productive enterprises, since decrease of income leads many individuals and families to increased effort to bring incomes up to a former standard. Since the opposite is likewise true in the case of other individuals and families, the demand for labor is affected by fluctuations of income from investment.

III. Labor is valued by undertakers, not in itself, but in its products. The price of products, however, gives us slight indications of what wages are or can be, since price must cover all costs of production, of which wages may be but a small part. The highest amount which can be paid will be much affected by the price of products in connection with the extent of the market, the technical skill of workmen, and the relation of efficiency to wages. Philippovich lays emphasis upon laborers' responsibility. Under normal circumstances, the most important element operating in the laborers' favor is the personal element. It is only by greater skill, greater industry, and greater care that their condition is elevated.

IV. Under "Ability to pay," little is said by this author. While accepting Hermann's view that undertakers stand between laborers and consumers of laborers' products, and that their ability to pay is affected by what consumers pay, he yet points out that undertakers may replenish their fund of disposable wage capital by means of credit. But how this fact may affect wages is not made clear. This is a point which has been mentioned by both Brentano and Philippovich, but has been left undeveloped by both.

V. To understand adequately how laborers compete with each other we must perceive that industry is carried on in branches and laborers are divided into groups, separated more or less completely by differences in skill, special aptitude and training. However, there are in all branches of industry occupations which require only ordinary skill or intelligence and hence can be filled by the common laborers of all branches. Here exists almost complete competition and the lowest wages prevail. As we ascend in the scale of skilled and special employments up to the liberal professions, we find more and more important the group formations. Even in groups there are forces at work which tend to break down the barriers to competition. One such force is the existence in modern times of extended enforced idleness. Such idleness, not accidental but largely the result of the unsteadiness of industrial evolution, impels men to seek new employments, thus breaking down former group arrangements. There is always a readjustment of employment after an extended period of enforced idleness. Under certain exceptional conditions there are natural limitations to competition. When unoccupied land is plentiful competition will cease at the point where wages sink to the level of what labor can make on such land. But this is not the law under ordinary circumstances. The openings to labor without capital are small in number. As a rule labor power without capital has no value to its owner.

VI. By the amount of labor offering service our author does not mean the number of persons seeking work. That is measured by the labor power and skill of laborers and the number of hours during which daily its labor power can be active. The only point made under this head beyond the foregoing definition is that relating to the correspondence between time and service. Up to a certain point as the hours of the working day are shortened the quality of the service per hour increases. No attempt is made to determine this point, but it is brought out that if this point of maximum service is passed in the direction of shorter hours, the effect is the same as if the number of workers were decreased.

VII. The laborer's valuation of his labor power may be affected by two circumstances. Under the exceptional conditions of the existence of large quantities of fertile unoccupied land accessible to laborers, wages cannot sink below the income obtainable by the laborer in independent undertaking. But under ordinary conditions the opportunities for independent undertaking without large capital are insignificant, so that from this standpoint labor power has no value to the owner. A basis for its valuation is found by recognizing the personality of the laborer. This appears by reason of the cost value of labor and the standard of life. The cost of labor is not so simple as might at first appear. Even a narrow view must include in addition to support during the time of work, costs of bringing up and development of the laborer, support during the period of old age, and a reserve as a provision against sickness and other causes of loss of employment. But the laborer as a human personality is more than an individual. He is also the father of a family; and no fair judgment of the value of labor can ignore that fact. That it is so often ignored is accounted for by our author by a reference to the strong competition of labor, and the admittance of women to men's employments. The question of costs is much influenced, whether as an individual or the head of a family, by the standard of life, which is defined as the expense which one is induced on the average to incur for the satisfaction of wants, in accordance with the habit and custom of the group to which one is attached by his calling; or shortly, support conformable to one's rank. This differs so much according to peoples, times, and places, that it is impossible to reduce the standard of life to any law. In general it may be said that much depends upon the position accorded to the laboring class in society and political life. The different amount of contact with other social strata and the means of culture become of prime importance. Of course, the standard of life is a powerful force among all classes of society; but that of the laboring class has a special interest to students of society, because the integrity of the standard has a more or less precarious support in their case, and a failure to maintain it may mean a real degradation. It is because laborers are affected in their social position and their respectability that such fierce opposition is made to wage reductions. It is only by raising the standard of life that we can have a permanent rise of wages.

VIII. Wages may be said to be affected by money in that wages fall if money increases in value, and vice versa. The cause is a double one. If money becomes dearer, other things, including labor, become cheaper; but in the face of a falling market, production tends to diminish, and thus the demand for labor is lessened. It will be noticed that this argument for the most part applies to money wages only, and, indeed, the treatment thus far contemplates no determination of commodity wages.

The entire treatment by Philippovich may be summarized as follows: Wages are determined by the combined action of the following forces: 1. The competition for labor is greater, the larger the number of employers. 2. The demand for labor depends partly upon the amount of land and capital which the owners employ in productive industry. This employment is favored by small owners. 3. Labor is largely valued according to the efficiency and skill of workmen. 4. The power to employ labor is affected by the degree in which undertakers can restore capital either from consumers' incomes or by the use of credit. 5. Laborers are limited in their competition against each other by social and industrial group arrangements. 6. The labor supply is influenced by the length of the working day. 7. Wages, in many instances, are largely determined by what laborers can make in independent undertakings, although ordinarily there are no lucrative independent undertakings open to them. 8. The standard of life is an ever active powerful force affecting the supply of labor.

These will be recognized as important elements, but the analysis would be much more complete if some attempt were made to measure the relative importance of the factors. Under given circumstances, some factors are peculiarly active, while others are quiescent. If we are not to be confused by a mass of meaningless details, we must know these facts.

There are still two points under dispute which Philippovich discusses briefly. They pertain to the effects of a supposed rise of wages.

I. May wages rise at the cost of the undertakers? To answer this question intelligently we must analyze the undertaker's income. It is in the aggregate composed of (1) wages of superintendence, (2) interest, (3) profit. A rise of wages at his cost would affect him, therefore, either as leader, capitalist, or speculator. We may assume that his first two functions cannot be affected by this cause except through the last. If a rise should occur at the cost of profits, the undertaker would be in a more unfavorable position than the ordinary capitalist, for the latter includes in the rate of interest insurance against risk. Such a position he would not endure permanently, and the only reason he might temporarily would be the inability to withdraw his capital. Moreover, no one would embark in industries in which such conditions prevailed, so that in course of time production would decline, and with a rise in price profits would become normal.

There are certain kinds of industries in which wages might rise with no unfavorable effect upon profits. Such are certain forms of monopoly, or industries for whose products there is a rising market, or those in which the costs of production decrease more rapidly than wages increase. In such cases the advantages could be appropriated by labor only through combination. Labor unions, as instruments to keep wages from falling, are beneficial under certain circumstances, both in competitive and monopolized undertakings. In the first, to prevent undertakers from lowering wages under the stress of competitive pressure among themselves; in the second, where there is no pressure of competition, to force those to allow better conditions who can but will not voluntarily do so.

II. It has sometimes been said that if wages should rise at the cost of consumers, laborers would be sufferers in the end. The argument is that by so much as prices rise, consumers, having fixed incomes, must curtail their consumption. This means a weakened purchasing power in certain directions, resulting in a decrease of production and a falling off in the demand for labor power. But this is a point to which Brentano paid special attention, and Philippovich, without mentioning his authority, employs Brentano's argument. It is simply that any loss of former consumers' purchasing power is fully made up by the new additional purchasing power of laborers whose wages have been increased. Philippovich, however, did not fail to notice that, if prices were increased by a rise of wages, laborers would lose a part of their wage advance by having to pay higher prices for consumption goods. He at the same time pointed out that they would not lose all their advance, since a part of the burden of higher prices would be borne by capitalists, land-owners and professional men.

The discussion of these two questions becomes clearer by noticing the views of Thornton, whom both Brentano and Philippovich are either following or criticising. Brentano would naturally consider Thornton, for his article in Hildebrand's Jahrbücher was devoted to a study of the doctrine of wage increase. Philippovich took up the discussion doubtless because he felt that no systematic work on Political Economy would be complete without it, although he had nothing especially new upon the subject.

Thornton[1] desired to determine whether trades unions could be instrumental in securing for laborers a permanent advance in wages above what would be secured without union action. He was met at the beginning of the discussion by the objection that whatever the unions might succeed in extorting would either have been granted eventually without union action or could not be lasting, according to circumstances.

The first objection was supported by the contention that if labor organizations should force a wage advance in some particular trade, at a time when business was improving and profits abnormally advancing in that same trade, it would be but to anticipate what must occur later by forces purely economic when capital should be attracted to that trade by reason of the extraordinary profits prevailing. The advent of new capital would cause an increase of demand for labor, and wages must rise in consequence. Thornton admitted the force of this argument,

[1] *On Labour*, p. 279–321.

but claimed that unless the unions intervened at the beginning of the process the employers would pocket the whole advantage during the time preceding the advent of competition. Furthermore, if laborers waited for competition to raise their wages they would suffer loss, for increased production following competition in production would lower prices, and thus the source of higher wages would be partially cut off. This point Philippovich also notes. So much for the efficiency of union action in case profits are above the general level.

The second objection that higher wages, extorted at a time when profits were at an equilibrium or were below the general level, could not be permanent, Thornton denied for the greater number of cases to which the rule was applicable. Unionism can raise wages permanently in the following cases: (1) Those in which there exists monopoly, for prices can be raised against consumers to meet the increased cost. (2) Those in which, whether monopolized or not, the demand of customers is increasing. Prices may be raised. (3) Those in which economizing machinery and processes are being introduced. By these means laborers are more efficient and a greater number of products at old prices is as beneficial to employers as the same number at higher prices. (4) A rise of wages is also possible if all trades were united in a combination so that an equal and simultaneous rise of wages would produce a universal fall of profits. In this case, capital having no place to which to flee for relief, must submit. There are other cases mentioned, but these are the more important. In all the cases mentioned above, except the third, higher wages are obtained only at the expense of undertakers or consumers. Indeed, Thornton lays it down as a general proposition that wages cannot rise except as prices rise or profits fall. Hence it becomes important to enquire: in all cases in which unionists are the gainers, who are the losers? This is, of course, a difficult problem, since all are consumers.

We shall indicate briefly Thornton's answer, as it is to his answer that the German economists take exception. He says that this will depend upon many circumstances, the important ones being, whether the gain has taken place in a competitive or in a monopolized trade, or whether it has taken place during a stationary or a progressive period. We will simply notice here the case of monopolized industries. If the rise occurs in such an industry in a prosperous period, employers are not injured, for they can raise the price. Consumers are the only positive losers; for, although they may be compelled to pay more for one class of commodities than formerly, they may still be able to spend as much as before on the produce of other trades. In that case laborers in general would not be deprived of anything they were accustomed to; "they would merely be excluded from participating in unaccustomed gains of which otherwise they would have had their share."

If a rise in wages is forced in monopolized industries during a period of stagnation, consumers are not the only losers. The main body of laborers, excluding those laborers the rise of whose wages is contemplated, are injured by the fact that the unionists have intercepted an amount of money which would otherwise have been expended in the purchase of commodities which the main body of laborers produces. In a stagnant period, incomes are regarded by Thornton as fixed; therefore, if the producers of one class of goods succeed in absorbing more than the former usual share of consumers' income, less remains for expenditure in other departments of trade. The curtailment of expenditure in these other directions diminishes demand for goods in these trades, and thus laborers employed in these trades are injured. Thus Thornton regarded the gain to a particular group of laborers under the circumstances noted above as offset by a double detriment; first to consumers, whose consumption was thereby curtailed, and secondly to the general body of laborers, the demand for whose products was thereby diminished.

This is the point to which both Brentano and Philippovich

object. As already noticed, they call attention to the increased purchasing power of the group of laborers whose wages by supposition have been increased. They would admit that consumers of the products whose price has been raised are sufferers, but they deny that the general body of laborers are necessarily affected. The aggregate demand for goods has not decreased because one class of consumers has benefited at the expense of another class. Laborers whose wages have been increased are more extensive consumers than formerly. They now possess an augmented purchasing power just equal to the diminished purchasing power of consumers affected by higher prices. The conclusion then is that when wages have been increased at the expense of consumers, the consumers are the chief sufferers, and that the general body of laborers are not affected by a diminution of demand for commodities. This view would doubtless have been admitted by Thornton if his attention had been called to it, for on its face there does not appear any reason why the general labor market need suffer because purchasing power has been transferred from one class of laborers to another.

If Philippovich corrected one of Thornton's errors, he did not avoid falling into another one of the same author. They both teach that in case of monopoly a rise of wages may occur at the expense of consumers. Both assume that monopolies have such control of the market that they can raise prices to meet extra expenses; thus there can be shifted upon consumers the burden of a higher wage cost. But if monopolists can increase prices to their advantage after a rise of wages, the question forces itself upon us as to why they could not do it before the event. Since precise studies have been made of the relation between the price of monopolised goods and monopoly profits, it seems clear that monopolists possess no power to shift upon consumers the burden of a higher wage rate. Monopolists always charge the highest price consumers are willing to pay. The principle of charge from the monopolist standpoint is the establishment of such a balance between costs and gross income as shall yield the highest net return. In general, the number of consumers of a particular good varies inversely as the price. An increase of wages constitutes an expense chargeable to an undertaking as an undivided whole, and is not one which varies with the amount of the commodity produced. Such a charge must be borne by the monopolist, for if he attempted to escape it by raising prices, consumption would be diminished so that the monopolist's net income would be decreased.

CHAPTER IV

CRITICISM

It is proposed now to discuss briefly two points pertaining to the work of this entire group, the centre of which is Hermann. The first point concerns the method of approaching the wages question by all the German economists from Rau to Philippovich. The characteristic method is to state that wages depend upon the law of supply and demand. In the same manner that that law determines the price of commodities, so with a few corrections it determines the price of labor. The reader of the German work on wages is referred to the analysis of supply and demand as applied to commodities, and then finds the author employing the same terminology, with here and there a word changed designed to suit the special case in hand.

The criticism of this method as applied by the group under consideration is that not sufficient emphasis is laid upon the very peculiar nature of labor as a commodity. This peculiar characteristic is illustrated by the application of the law of supply and demand to different kinds of exchangeable values, and by the analogy that may be drawn between labor power and certain kinds of goods.

If we undertake to rely upon the operation of demand and supply as a practical rule to regulate prices in all industries and for all services, we shall find that the rule does not apply with equal facility. The law of supply and demand as a regulator of price can be applied with the least advantage with regard to goods or utilities which are produced by a body of capital that can be easily, and with small loss by the change, increased or diminished. Such would be the case with capital invested in the stock exchange or in banking. Supply and demand have somewhat less application in a merchant's business, still less in manufacturing, and least of all in transportation, especially railroad transportation.[1] Banking, trading, manufacturing, and railroad transportation constitute a series of undertakings, at one end of which, banking, the principles of supply and demand in regulating price from the standpoint of costs, apply with the most satisfactory results; and at the other end these principles have less validity. In the banking business, nearly all the capital is circulating capital, but in the railroad business a larger proportion is fixed, and these opposed conditions make a great difference in the practical working out of prices. In the banking business, under free competition, if the price goes much above the costs of production, the unusual profits attract capital into the business till an equilibrium is established. If prices fall below costs of production, further production ceases till the equilibrium is again restored, and thus prices hover close to costs. Of the whole capital invested, the greater the proportion that is fixed, the more difficult it is to adjust investment to change of price. When it comes to a business like the railroad business, the costs of production or the cost of service have but slight influence upon charges. If competition forces prices below costs, there is no economic force to restore it, except such as work through long periods. In a merchant's business, sales below cost cause a greater loss the greater the amount of sales. But in the railroad traffic, any business that pays more than immediate expenses is worth more than no business. When a merchant becomes bankrupt he ceases to compete. But a bankrupt railroad is a more dangerous competitor than a sound road. In a merchant's business the law of supply and demand may be relied upon to adjust prices for the best good of the com-

[1] *Hadley, Railroad Transportation*, p. 40.

munity. But in the railroad business combination and agreement seem the only means to avoid industrial warfare.

Now the question occurs, is labor power, as a commodity, analogous to bank service or merchants' goods, or is it more analogous to factory products and railroad service? This is important, because upon the answer will depend the extent to which we can wisely and without great modification employ the same analysis of supply and demand that might be employed in reference to competitive goods. The laborer, for the purpose contemplated, now occupies the same position in relation to his labor power that the business man or capitalist does to the commodity or utility he produces. The laborer's capital is himself. As the business man maintains his capital only by producing and selling the utility his capital is fitted to produce, so the laborer is maintained by exercising and selling his labor power. The kinds of business referred to above as a series differ in two respects. First, in the ability to cease producing without serious detriment to the investment. Secondly, in the freedom and ease of transferring the value of the investment. In these two particulars banking is at one extreme of the series and the railroad business at the other. A banker may cease discounting without serious injury to the plant, and may easily close up business entirely, transferring the value of the capital to another business. A railroad cannot cease transporting without serious losses in fixed charges and in deterioration. It is comparatively useless as a body of mere property. Nearly all the value is in the business, so that it is next to impossible to decrease the supply of transportation according to the demand for it at old prices. The supply is kept up at such prices as will secure business. With reference to these last points labor is more analogous to the railroad business than to banking.[1] A laborer cannot cease selling his product without serious, and it may be permanent, detriment to

[1] *Hadley, Railroad Transportation*, p. 78.

his investment, that is himself. And here the laborer's position is peculiar, in that he carries upon his shoulders, so to speak, the future supply of labor. If his labor should cease, not only is his own investment damaged, but that of others who are dependent upon him. It is as if a business were being conducted not alone for the sake of the owner, but also as a support for the business of others, so that if the one ceases the others of necessity fall also.

Neither is the laborer free to withdraw his capital and produce something else. The laborer never has anything to sell except labor power. If capital does not wish to buy what he offers for sale, there is no hope for it. Capital buys at some price or the laborer goes to the poor-house. These two considerations make it as impossible for labor to cease selling its product, as for a railroad to cease running its trains.

This analysis discloses the peculiar nature of labor-power as a commodity. Its immobility is a serious obstacle to the reduction of wages to a common level. Its comparatively permanent supply, together with its necessary productive activity, retards the correcting power of supply and demand. We may say that the operation of the law of supply and demand in its application to labor is greatly impeded by friction. And in any practical treatment of the wages question such as is found in the German literature, the friction-element ought to dominate the discussion more than it does.

None of the authors of this group take pains to point out these characteristic differences between labor and competitive commodities except Philippovich. But the differences discussed by him have slight effect upon his subsequent treatment. Rau designated an upper and lower limit of price, and appealed to supply and demand as forces operating to determine wages at some definite figure between those limits. But the result is vague and indefinite. Hermann employed the familiar procedure, but omitted a discussion of that part of the question which, according to his method, would have given him an opportunity to point out the comparatively permanent character of the supply of labor. Having, however, placed wages in the same category as the prices of commodities, he practically sets aside all factors as having no force except consumers' income. Although his followers, for the most part, enter upon the discussion of wages by an elaboration of factors identical with those applied to determine the prices of commodities, they ultimately appeal to some one as really final. When this is not done, as in the case of Philippovich, the whole treatment is confused. All recent writers practically adopt Hermann's view. It is desirable, therefore, to enter upon some discussion of consumers' income as the source and determinant of general wages, and this is the second point in the criticism.

It will be recalled that Adam Smith pointed out that there was necessarily a minimum rate, below which it seemed impossible that even the lowest grade of labor could subsist for any considerable period of time. This lowest rate for any family must be more than sufficient to support the man and wife. When it went below this, it failed to be consistent with the needs of common humanity, and had the effect of producing a dearth of workmen. However, the possibility of raising wages above the minimum depended upon the increase of the "funds" which are "destined for the payment of wages." These funds were of two kinds: first, the revenue which is over and above what is necessary for the maintenance of the employer, and secondly, capital which is over and above what is necessary in order that the employer may conduct his business on any given scale. In the first part of the section on wages, he showed that wages were the result of a contract entered into by laborers and employers. In settling the terms of the contract, the employers have the advantage. In the long run, laborers may be as necessary to employers as employers are to laborers, but, practically speaking, it cannot be a question of "long run" with workmen. Employers could subsist for a long time on present accumulations. "Many workmen could not subsist a week, few could subsist a month, and scarce any a year, without employment."[1] Notwithstanding the fact, however, that employers have the advantage, wages for the most part are above the minimum, and this fact is not to be regretted; for good wages, by increasing the efficiency of workmen, redound to the distinct advantage of society. Some modification of this last proposition is necessary, since there are two kinds of laborers corresponding to the two kinds of funds for the payment of wages: (1) Laborers who are paid from stock are such as by their exertions add to the wealth of society. They are "productive." (2) Laborers who are paid from revenue and render services simply. They minister to personal enjoyment, but their product perishes with the first use, and there is added nothing to social wealth. Such labor is "unproductive." Adam Smith makes it clear that productive processes extend over periods of time, and that wages are advanced to laborers by the owners of wealth as the result of a bargain. But the exact nature of the funds held by employers is not made lucid.[2] Thus there are two theories of wages in the Wealth of Nations. One is the minimum wage theory, the other is the theory of demand and supply, the latter connected with the idea of funds for the payment of wages.

Ricardo's treatment differed somewhat from Adam Smith's. The minimum wage is with Ricardo the natural price of labor, a reward which is "necessary to enable the laborers, one with another, to subsist, and to perpetuate their race, without either increase or diminution." Any deviation from this rate, by the operation of supply and demand is called a "market" rate. The laborers are in a flourishing and happy condition if the market rate is above the natural rate, and in a "most wretched" condition if it is below the natural rate. This statement is

[1] Rogers' 2d ed., v. 1, p. 70.

[2] Taussig, *Wages and Capital*, p. 150.

much qualified by Ricardo later, either in statement or in emphasis, as follows:

1. The "natural" rate is not to be understood as absolutely fixed. The habits and customs of the people make a difference between different nations, and between different periods of the same nation.

2. Notwithstanding the statement of the importance of the standard of life, it is practically ignored in the subsequent discussions on taxation, and the general problems of distribution.

3. Market wages seem to have small interest to Ricardo, probably because natural wages furnished the key to distribution.

Revenue nowhere appears as playing a part in the demand for labor. He took into consideration only those laborers who are hired by capitalists with a view to realize on the investment, and so far as market wages are considered, he regards them as determined by the relation of capital and population. In his essay "On the Influence of the Low Price of Corn on the Profits of Stock," Ricardo says that the rise or fall of wages in the stationary state is regulated wholly by the increase or decrease of the population. In the advancing state it depends on whether the capital or population advance at the more rapid course. In the retrograde state it depends upon whether population or capital decrease with the greater rapidity.[1]

As the income mentioned by Adam Smith was that of the employer, and in his view would exercise influence on wages only so far as it was used to employ domestic servants, the income side of Adam Smith's wages-fund would be naturally neglected so soon as writers come to regard the most important case of wages as arising when men were employed for a profit. Neglected it certainly was and, if for the reason stated above, the negligence is justified. But viewing Economics from the side of production, and production from the

[1] *Works*, p. 379.

side of capital, English writers were led away from consumption and the demand of consumers as leaders in economic activity. It is at this point that Hermann made a departure from the traditions of the science, and intercepted the parallel course of thinking on wages in England and Germany. Capital is repudiated as the source and determinant of wages. The key to the situation is no longer held by the employers but by the consumers. Employers are mere agents, middlemen, who do the consumers' bidding for a commission. The consumer is the real buyer of labor. All the steps leading to the final product are taken for the final consumer. The true and continuous source of compensation for production is the income of the buyer of the product for his own use.

This doctrine has been followed generally by the German economists; but in England it has not received very strong support. In the first place, Mill attacked its main position in his famous proposition that a demand for commodities is not a demand for labor. Mill thought it important to support this proposition because its contrary was so widely assumed by common apprehension; and because, with the exception of Say and Ricardo, most economists fell into the error in some part of their thinking. Up to Mill's time, however, it formed no integral part of their theories of wages. Although of late some of Mill's reasoning on this point is not accepted, the whole of it passed practically unchallenged for twenty years. In the second place, when Longe and Thornton adopted Hermann's point of view, and tried to persuade their countrymen of its soundness, with some success, if judged by Mill's action, Cairnes submitted the doctrine to a careful analysis and published the results in the form of an elaborate attack in his "Some Leading Principles in Political Economy Newly Expounded."

There is something very plausible in the idea that demand for commodities determines the aggregate amount of wealth spent in wages. It is of a kind with the popular conviction that the "extravagance of the rich is the gain of the poor," or that "profusion is for the good of trade."[1]

The source of the error, as to wages, seems to be the failure to distinguish between general and particular wages, wages of all laborers and those of groups of laborers. The discussions on wages are for the most part grouped about three questions: (1) What is the true source of the quantity of real goods which laborers as a body receive? (2) What determines the quantity? (3) What determines the share of any particular group? Let us consider briefly these questions in the order stated.

I. It is evident that it is from the total productions of society that ultimately all wages must come. It is also evident that, under our present system, wages cannot absorb the whole of that product. The first difference of opinion appears when the attempt is made to designate the particular part of this total product which furnishes wages, or the habitual form which it assumes as a source of wages.

All goods have a career. For some, the career is short, for others long; some are destined to give direct enjoyment to society, others to help in the process of production. The tracing of the career of goods is a comparatively simple process. Under our wage system they are first in the hands of the entrepreneur class, then in those of the trading classes, and finally in those of the consumers or users. To be sure, some goods suffer destruction by fire and some by accident, while some may revert to the trading classes as second-hand goods; but if they fulfill their proper destiny, they finally disappear in the users' hands. There is a continual inflow at the one end of the line, and a continual outflow at the other. The complication comes when we attempt to note the causes which determine the positions which classes hold with reference to the flow and ebb of goods, and the relations of the classes to each other as an outcome of the various positions. Could we cause the economic

[1] Cairnes, *Political Economy*, p. 163.

flux and the social flux to cease for a time while we noted the various positions of goods and classes, we would find some goods just issuing forth, others passing away, still others in all stages of intermediate progress. We should also find all classes of men concerned with the dissipation of goods in the process of what we call consumption. There is great diversity in the value of goods thus consumed, as also in the economy and profuseness of consumption.

Of these some take no part whatever in the inflow of goods. Of those who do, we distinguish (1) the so-called small producer who combines his labor with some accumulation in the production of goods; (2) those who have large accumulations of their own, or that which belongs to others; (3) those who have little or no accumulation, and are employed by the second class. The problem of distribution is a study of the causes which determine, for final consumption, the proportionate assignment of the total productions of society to social classes. And the wage problem, as a part of the question of distribution, so far as the source of wages is concerned, is a double one. 1st, To what stage must products arrive before they become the source of wages? 2d, Into the possession of what class must they come to be such a source? Some hold that the source of wages is a portion of wealth held by employers in its form of food (capital); others that part which the laborers have immediately helped to produce (product); still others that part held by dealers of commodities in the form of laborers' consumption goods held for sale, *i. e.*, capital in the hands, not of employers, but of merchants; and, finally, some regard it as that part of wealth which is, or is about to be, in the hands of the consumers of laborers' product as a money income. Hermann and his followers, of course, are identified with the last view.

II. The second question pertains to the determination of the quantity of real goods going to labor. As men differ in regard to the source of wages, so they differ as to the cause of the amount. Those who look to the employers' capital as the source, think that the state of the arts principally determines what portion of total capital shall be used to employ labor. This determines the sum total that can be divided among laborers. Those who look to labor's product as the source, lay stress upon labor's efficiency or productivity as chiefly fixing the quantity. Here the element of time is important, for in short periods contract may prevent an adjustment to efficiency. A perfect competition on the part of capitalists is alsc postulated in order that interest may be kept at a minimum rate and prevented from absorbing the share of laborers. Those who look to merchants' capital as the source of real wages make the volume of the flow of consumable goods to laborers dependent upon the volume of money wages. Such wages are in general dependent upon employers' means. Hence a rise in wages, other things being equal, can occur only if the directors of industry are able to add to their money resources and enlarge their undertakings. Finally, those who appeal to the income of consumers rest their case upon the assumption of a more or less definite proportion between wages and consumers' income. This is also the point of view of Hermann and his followers. For completeness there ought to be some attempt to distinguish between the power of consumption of laborers and that of other classes, and the extent to which laborers are the consumers of their own products. On the most superficial view, it must appear that laborers and their families, constituting as they do a considerable proportion of the population, are large consumers of their own products. Just in so far as this is true, wages appears as a determinant of itself, and thus we reason in a circle. Hermann did not escape this kind of reasoning, though Brentano did.

III. Writers on wages have not always distinguished between general wages and group wages. Some have evolved a theory explanatory of the wages of laborers as one body opposed to all other classes. They have determined certain principles applicable to the larger problem, and then have proceeded to draw certain conclusions about the wages of groups based upon those principles, without perceiving the change of problem. Others have pursued the opposite policy. Having perhaps correctly observed the relation of cause and effect in the case of wages of groups, the principles so evolved are likewise used as a solution of the other problem, which is so different. Hermann and his followers seem to be guilty of this last error. They observed that individual employers enter upon industry with a view to gain profit, that they regulate their production by their customers' demands. If demand increases, more is invested; if demand falls, less is invested. This increase or decrease of investment carries with it corresponding changes in the amount paid in wages. As individual employers do, all do; therefore wages depend ultimately upon consumers' demand.

If we have regard to a single industry, it seems clear that the investment of capital and the total amount paid in wages follow closely the lead of consumers' demand. There can be little question but that it is effective in distributing the relative amounts of capital over the whole field of production. Production is for no other purpose than to meet the varying demands of men, and capital is ever on the alert to anticipate, if possible, the growing and changing wants of humanity. There is thus a re-shifting of industry and employment, and wages are sensibly affected, at least for short periods. However, even here it can scarcely be said that demand determines the amount of investment. What it does is to influence it more or less. These matters are important as throwing light on the determination of group wages. But the problem of general wages is a different one. Here we view income as a whole, and industry as a total. The effectual demand of society is the offer of total income. We are unable to conceive of an increase or decrease of demand without at the same time conceiving an increase or decrease of production. In the view of Hermann, an increased demand is viewed as a cause of which increased investment and increased production is the effect. While viewing total demand and total production, increased production must ever be the cause of increased demand. We see, therefore, how unfitted this theory is as an explanation of general wages, although it may throw light on particular wages.[1]

[1] See Cairnes, *Political Economy*, and Taussig, *Wages and Capital*.

CHAPTER IV

VON THÜNEN

Johann Heinrich von Thünen, born 1783, died 1850, was a Mecklenburg aristocrat who, as a scientific land cultivator, endeavored to put to a test, on his own property, the theoretical conclusions of his economic studies. He is regarded by the Germans as their most original theoretical economist. As a close student of English political economy he professed to have little confidence in its conclusions; yet he did not succeed in emancipating himself from either the characteristic method, or some of the more important results of his English preceptors. There runs through his thinking on the subject of wages the fundamental assumption that neither wages nor interest can rise except at the expense of the other. They are supplied from a fixed amount, and whatever causes a rise in one must produce a corresponding fall in the other. He proceeds, as Smith and Ricardo, did by assuming simple primitive conditions or hypothetical cases. His method is wholly deductive and highly abstract.

Thünen's confidence in future economic peace is disturbed by his belief that the laborer is separated from the results of his productive power.[1] It was his opinion that, so long as such a state of things lasts, hostility between labor and capital is inevitable and not without justification. Under present arrangements labor does not get all it produces, but there is no reason in justice why it should not. It is not enough to ask what wages are. We must enquire what wages ought to be.

[1] *Der Isolirte Staat*, ii, p. 210.

Wages are, roughly speaking, determined by the relation of supply and demand, and under this influence they tend to the standard of life minimum. This point is treated in a most original manner, if we remember that it was written in the early part of this century. Business men will employ additional laborers up to the point at which the last laborer employed produces his own wages; beyond that they cannot go without loss; to that point self-interest prompts them to go. Under the operation of competition all laborers of like grade receive the same wages as the last one employed. If at this point all are miserable, what remedy is there? The undertaker cannot be blamed, for, while he may make a surplus from the earlier laborers employed, to suppose that he will bestow it as a free gift to his laborers is to fail to distinguish between moral obligations and business principles. A rise in wages without a decrease in the number of laborers employed is not possible, for then the last employed laborer produces less than his wages. Employers must discharge men until wages equal production. On the other hand, rather than remain breadless, discharged men are willing to work at a figure which makes their employment possible. If we suppose an increase in the number of laborers without a corresponding increase of capital and land, wages must fall, for the undertaker can employ additional labor only on less productive objects. If laborers increase, in spite of sinking wages, the only limit to population is the means of subsistence. How productive the object is upon which the last laborer is employed depends upon the supply of labor. The greater the supply of labor, the less productive will the capital be upon which the last laborer employed works. To what limit wages may sink depends upon the sum of the means of subsistence. Between the real worth of labor, the supply of labor, and the means of subsistence of labor there is an intimate connection. The economists have considered the last two factors only, and have thereby drawn the conclusion that

Providence has designed for laborers nothing except necessary support during the period of their life.[1] Such a conclusion can not be admitted, and will be found to be scientifically untenable when we have investigated the real worth of labor.

Von Thünen complained that Adam Smith's law of the relation of supply and demand as determining wages was dependent upon changes in the national wealth. He desired to discover a law of wages for a persistent condition of society. In such a condition, demand and supply are in equilibrium; each cancels the other. Since they appear to be inactive, there must be some other law. To the question, what is the natural share of the laborer in products brought forth by him, Adam Smith answers, that which he usually gets. But that which he usually gets through competition is subject to continual change. We must ask which one of all those actually received is the right one, the natural one. Adam Smith did not investigate this question.[2]

If we compare von Thünen's conception of natural wages with that of Ricardo's, we find them quite different. Ricardo was the analyst of actual economic facts. In the realm of distribution he sought to establish no reform. Hence he offered no criticisms of the social method of awarding shares. To his mind the essential task at that time was to establish, if possible, beyond all question, what the social method actually was. He found it convenient to adopt Adam Smith's distinction between wages which fluctuate in short periods according to the varying strength of demand for labor, and wages which prevail in the long run and are connected with the decrease or increase of population. Ricardo called wages natural which enabled laborers under the influence of climate and habit to perpetuate their kind without increase or diminution. Von Thünen's interest in economic questions was different.

[1] *Der Isolirte Staat*, ii, p. 86–90.

[2] *Der Isolirte Staat*, ii, p. 64.

He was not less keenly alive than Ricardo to the importance of a theoretical statement of actual distribution, and in this field he achieved probably as notable success. But he brooded over the miseries of the poor, and sought for the causes in the national economic system. To him a wage which was divorced from correspondence with production was unjust and unnatural. In a word, he called wages natural when they were in agreement with justice; and justice required that a man should be rewarded according to his production. But in seeking the law of wages the interests of both capitalists and laborers must be taken into account.

To eliminate the complicating effect of rent, von Thünen seized upon the idea of the isolated community. He supposes a large city situated in the centre of a fruitful plain. To eliminate unnecessary causes of unequal opportunity, he supposes the plain not crossed by river or canal. At a considerable distance from the city the plain ends in a wilderness which wholly separates the supposed state from the rest of the world. All laborers are equally strong, wise and skillful. The number of laborers remains the same, *i. e.*, there are just enough children brought to maturity to fill the ranks depleted by age and death. The population is also so limited that plenty of land awaits occupation. Hence there is a border where no rent is paid, for rather than pay rent the *Bauer* would take new land. Conditions on the border determine for the entire community what wages shall be paid, for there wages are not determined by the will of the employer, the competition of laborers, or the means of subsistence, but by what the laborer can himself produce. Such wages are paid throughout the entire community by the force of competition. Conditions on the border also determine interest, since there capital has its highest uses, and being highly volatile, it finds the place of highest reward. Von Thünen was careful to credit as much to interest as belonged to it. Not all that falls into laborers' hands, ostensibly as wages, is properly to be considered as such. Nearly all workmen are furnished with equipment of one sort and another, such as implements or tools to assist them in labor, and a part of what they receive is to be accredited to interest for their use.

In order that labor may not be at the mercy of competition, he supposes conditions under which labor may freely apply itself to unoccupied land. An investigation as to how high wages may be under these conditions will teach us what natural wages are, for here the laborer will get what belongs to him. The total product is divided between two claimants: laborers and capitalists. It will be found that the interests of both are best subserved when the so-called natural wages are paid. The problem, then, is to determine the relation of the rate of wages to the rate of interest. This Von Thünen attempts to do by reducing the efficiency of capital to labor-terms. It involves the most difficult problem of determining the shares attributable to labor and capital out of a product which is the result of the two in co-operation. Before entering upon this discussion, it will be perhaps best to give some explanation of the mathematical terms employed.

A represents the wages for the year of a family, including the wife and young children under fourteen years old. These wages are expressed in bushels of rye. To determine how much such a family would consume would manifestly depend upon the number of children. In this investigation it is von Thünen's aim to find a law for the regulation of wages and rate of interest for the stationary state of society; hence the working population is supposed to be constant. Each family will therefore on the average succeed in raising a sufficient number of children to replace the losses by age and death. The necessaries of life, which are required to keep such an average family in labor power for a year, are assumed to be such value as is equal to the value of a bushel of rye. If from the total wages A the necessaries be subtracted, there will be a surplus which is designated by the letter y. Then

$A = a + y$. That part of the gross product which is left after deducting repairs of all sorts, costs of raw material, and administration, as well as profits to the undertaker as such, is called by Thünen the "product of labor." This is a technical expression, as evidently the product is the joint result of the cooperation of labor and capital. If we divide the product of labor by the number of laborers employed, we get the amount of the labor-product of one man, which is designated by "p."

We now turn to the reduction of the efficiency of capital to labor-terms, and it is necessary to follow our author somewhat closely. If we suppose a capital Q and a wage $a + y$ expressed in bushels of rye, dollars, or any other measure of value, and that Q be divided by $a + y$, we have as a result an expression for capital in terms of the year's labor of a family, or we have discovered how many years' labor of a family a capitalist with Q capital can employ.[1] If this labor quantity be represented by nq, then $\frac{Q}{a+y} = nq$, and $Q = nq(a + y)$. If $a + y$ be regarded as equivalent to a unit of capital, then $Q = nq$ units of capital. In case the capitalist lends his capital to an undertaker who employs n laborers, then each laborer is assisted by $\frac{nq}{n} = q$ capital. The product of a laborer employed with a capital q for a year is designated by "p;" p, then, is a joint product, and the problem is to find an equitable division between the laborer and capitalist. If n laborers are employed, the product of all laborers is np; their wages are $n(a + y)$; the capitalist has the difference: $np - n(a + y) = n(p - [a + y])$. The capital employed is $nq(a + y)$. If the rate of interest be designated by z, then $z = \frac{n(p - [a + y])}{nq(a + y)} = \frac{p - (a + y)}{q(a + y)}$. The *laborer's share* can now be expressed in terms of labor-product, rate of interest, and capital.

[1] *Der Isolirte Staat*, ii, p. 124.

From $z = \frac{p-(a+y)}{q(a+y)}$ is obtained $qz(a+y) = p-(a+y)$; from this is obtained the following:

$$(1 + qz)(a + y) = p; \text{ whence}$$

$$a + y = \frac{p}{1 + qz} = \text{laborer's share.}$$

The *capitalist's share* is found by subtracting the laborer's share from the product of labor:

$$p - \frac{p}{1 + qz} = \frac{p + pqz - p}{1 + qz} = \frac{p(qz)}{1 + qz} = \text{capitalist's share.}$$

From the above it appears that the relation of the laborer's share to that of the capitalist is as $1 : qz$. This relation may be variously expressed: The reward of q units of capital equals the wages of qz laborers, and the reward of one unit of capital is equal to the wages of z laborers, or as is subsequently required in the discussion: The wages of one year's labor are to the earnings of q units of capital as 1 is to qz, or the wages of one year's labor are to the earnings of one unit of capital as 1 is to z.

Von Thünen has now succeeded in finding a mathematical expression for the relation of the reward of capital and labor. He must proceed one step further to express the relation of their efficiencies. Since in the production of one and the same product p, a part of the capital may be replaced by labor and *vice versa*, it appears that each is a competitor of the other. It is therefore in the power of the undertaker who with Q capital hires, say n laborers, to give any desirable value to q by increase or decrease of the number of laborers. The undertaker who knows and follows his interest will raise q to the point where capital-cost and labor-cost are in direct relation to the efficiency of both. Hence the reward of both capital and labor is measured by the efficiency of each.[1] If the reward of labor is to the reward of capital as 1 is to z, and the efficiency of labor is to the efficiency of capital as the reward of labor is to

[1] *Der Isolirte Staat*, ii, p. 126.

the reward of capital, then the efficiency of labor is to the efficiency of capital as 1 is to z. We arrive, then, at the following very important conclusion: When capital and human labor are measured by the same rule, viz., the year's labor of an individual man, the rate of interest, "z," is the factor by which the relation of the efficiency of capital and that of labor is expressed. By this we can reduce to labor terms the co-operation of capital in the production of goods. Furthermore, in so far as land rent does not enter, it is possible by this to express in terms of labor the cost of production of a commodity, and thereby labor becomes a true measure of the value of goods.[1]

The place which the "reduction of the efficiency of capital to labor-terms" has in the general discussion will be more clearly seen later on. Von Thünen has to exercise constant care that at every step in the process no unknown term shall be allowed to do duty for known ones. He started out to obtain an expression for natural wages. He has obtained an expression for wages under existing conditions with which he cannot rest, for it contains too many unknown quantities. In the expression $a+y=\frac{p}{1+qz}$ the value of $a+y$ is dependent upon the value of z, so that to get the value of $a+y$ we must know the value of z. Now p is not constant, but increases and diminishes with the value of q and is therefore dependent upon it. Upon the value of p depends again the value of y and z. Therefore p, y and z are functions of q. The problem therefore is to find the value of p, y and z for a given value of q.[2] He then turns to his favorite hypothetical society in paragraph 14, in which he says that it is on the margin of cultivation of the isolated state that we are to find the conditions for the development of the relation between wages and the rate of interest.[3] Here it is possible to be free from the confusion

[1] *Der Isolirte Staat*, ii, p. 127.

[2] *Ibid.*, p. 139.

[3] *Ibid.*, p. 140.

due to the presence of land rent. Here laborers are free to choose whether they will continue as wage laborers or move to unoccupied land and lay out a property of their own. If laborers are to be kept as farm hands, their total income, made up of wages and interest upon capital required to lay out a farm, must equal the product of labor procurable from a marginal farm which they might themselves have laid out.[1] Von Thünen expresses this mathematically. If wages $= a + y$, product of labor $= p$ and the capital required to lay out a small farm $=$ $q(a+y)$—all expressed in bushels of rye—and the rate of interest $= z$ per cent., then that laborers may be retained the following equation must hold: $a + y + q(a+y)z = p$. From this results: $a + y = \frac{p}{1 + qz}$; and $z = \frac{p - (a+y)}{q(a+y)}$. In this expression under the conditions assumed a, p and q are constant quantities, only y and z being variable. It is of the first importance to find the exact relation between y and z, for upon that solution depends a knowledge of the relation between wages and interest.[2] He then undertakes to find an expression for y which does not contain the quantity for z.

He supposes that a number of laborers form a combination on the margin of cultivation of the isolated state to put into cultivation a new farm. That there may be no disadvantage attached to this farm on account of its size, it is supposed to be as large as the average in the state. The laborers united for this purpose divide themselves into two groups. Group I is busied preparing the land for cultivation, erecting buildings, etc. Group II is composed of men who for the time being remain as laborers for hire, and by means of the surplus which they have above that required for their own support, offer the means of support of Group I. Under these conditions, says von Thünen, in the preparation of the farm, none of the existing national capital is consumed. The sum of those

[1] *Der Isolirte Staat*, ii, p. 141. [2] *Ibid.*, p. 142.

objects of value after completing the farm is as great as before its completion. The new farm has cost labor, and nothing but labor.[1] These two groups of laborers have really devoted their surplus to the production of this farm, and the farm may be spoken of as their invested capital, the interest of which must come from the future products of the farm. Groups I and II are called throughout von Thünen's discussion "capital producing laborers." Now the question occurs, how shall the wages of farm hands be determined? Von Thünen answers that it must be sufficiently high so that the surplus of a laborer put out at interest will equal the interest of a "capital producing laborer;" for if this were not the case the laborers would immediately go to capital producing. It is the interest of each, both laborers and capitalists, to get as high a return as possible, but there is no opposition between the two classes. In economic life, as we know it, if efficiency is not affected by changes in wages, capitalists' interests are promoted by lowering wages; but, under the simple conditions which von Thünen supposes, this does not follow. As will be more clearly seen later on, the following question is to the point: what rate of wages can capitalists pay and draw the highest rate of interest, supposing the efficiency is not considered, and that capitalists were to have the same rate of wages when they were producing capital? To show what he means by this question, and also as an aid in the solution of the same, it will be necessary to recur once more to his use of mathematical symbols. n represents the number of labor families whose continuous labor is required to cultivate the farm after its preparation. nq represents the number of laborers in Group I. In this expression is included the cooperation of capital.[2] A laborer employed with q capital produces p, and the product of n laborers equals np. Group I has in the course of the year consumed anq bushels of rye.

[1] *Der Isolirte Staat*, ii, p. 151.

[2] *Ibid.*, ii, p. 152.

Since Group II devotes its surplus to the support of Group I there are as many laborers in Group II as the number of times that y, the surplus of each man, is contained in anq, the amount consumed, hence the expression $\frac{anq}{y}$. The whole number of "capital producing laborers" then is $nq + \frac{anq}{y} = nq\frac{a+y}{y}$. The entire wage expense for farm cultivation is $n(a+y)$. If we subtract this outlay from the total product np we have $np - n(a+y) = n(p - [a+y])$. It is the yearly product of the farm, which belongs to $nq\frac{a+y}{y}$ and is their profit, or interest on the capital invested. To find each man's share we only need to divide the farm profit by the number of owners. Therefore $\frac{n(p-[a+y])}{nq\frac{a+y}{y}} = \frac{n(p-[a+y])y}{nq(a+y)}$ equals each man's share.

The question next occurs: how is the share of each "capital-producing laborer" affected by changes in the rate of wages? It is here assumed that the requirements of life, "a," remain the same, and that any change in wages affects y, the surplus only. It will be seen[1] that changes in y result in contrary effects upon each capital producer's share. First, an increase or decrease of y is equivalent to an increase or decrease in the cost of the cultivation of the farm. So far an increase of y works to the detriment of each man's share, and a decrease of y works in favor of each man's share. Second, on the other hand, an inspection of the expression for Group I reveals the fact that an increase of y results in a decrease of the number of owners, with a resulting increase in each man's share. The decrease of y gives a contrary result. Hence changes in y work double and opposite results. It follows that there must

[1] See table below, p. 79.

be a fixed amount for the labor surplus at which the profit share reaches its maximum amount. Von Thünen shows by means of the following table how—the product 300 c being unaffected, the wages increasing—the profit share is affected, supposing the number of laborers to remain a constant:

Where $a=100$, $a+y$ equals	Capital in Group II reduced to labor. $q=12$ y'rs l.	Capital in Group I reduced to labor. $\frac{aq}{y}$ year's labor.	Sum of labor in Groups I and II. $\frac{q(a+y)}{y}$	Interest on farm investment. $p-(a+y)$	A single capitalist receives $\frac{p-[a+y]y}{q(a+y)}$
120 c	12	$\frac{100 \times 12}{20} = 60$	$\frac{12(100+20)}{20} = 72$	$300c - 120c = 180c$	$\frac{300c\,[100+20]20}{12(100+20)} = 2.5c$
150 c	12	$\frac{100 \times 12}{50} = 24$	36	150 c	4.16 c
180 c	12	$\frac{100 \times 12}{80} = 15$	27	120 c	4.44 c
210 c	12	$\frac{100 \times 12}{110} = 10.9$	22.9	90 c	3.91 c
240 c	12	$\frac{100 \times 12}{140} = 8.57$	20.57	60 c	2.92 c
270 c	12	$\frac{100 \times 12}{170} = 7.06$	19.06	30 c	1.57 c
300 c	12	$\frac{100 \times 12}{200} = 6$	18	0	0

It is seen that the total number of "capital producing laborers" decreases with the increase of y because a smaller number of Group II is required to support Group I. We see, too, that total farm profit decreases because the more the laborers take from a constant product, the less is the remainder. The profit share of each man increases for a time, but later diminishes till finally the farm laborers get all that is produced. This gives the conclusion again that there must be a point in the amount of wages where the profit share is the highest. The specific question is: what value shall y have in order that the profit share $\frac{p-([a+y])y}{q(a+y)}$ shall have its maximum value? This is a question for the calculus. Accordingly $\frac{p-([a+y])y}{q(a+y)}$ must be differentiated with respect to y and the differentiation placed equal to o.

$$d\left[\frac{(p-[a+y])y}{q(a+y)}\right]=d\frac{(py-ay-y^2)}{q(a+y)}$$

$$=q(a+y)(p-a-2y)dy-(py-ay-y^2)qdy=0$$

$$\text{therefore } (a+y)(p-a-2y)=py-ay-y^2$$

$$ap-a^2-2ay+py-ay-2y^2=py-ay-y^2$$

$$ap-a^2-2ay-2y^2=-y^2$$

$$y^2+2ay=ap-a^2$$

$$(a+y)^2=ap$$

$$a+y=\sqrt{ap}$$

Expressed in words this means that it is in the interest of capitalists that wages be equal to the square root of the product of the necessaries of life and the product result of labor, all expressed in some common measure. Such a wage, not determined by supply and demand, or springing from the necessities of the laborer, but from the free determination of the laborer, von Thünen calls natural wages.[1]

This discussion, so far, aims to show that it is in the interest of the "capital producing laborers" that wages be $\sqrt{ap}$. If it can be shown that laborers themselves receive the highest amount as interest upon the investment of their surplus when wages are $\sqrt{ap}$, the claim that it is the natural wage has some reinforcement. He proceeds to show this in the following manner: According to a former expression (see p. 76) $(1+qz)(a+y)=p$, whence $a+y=\frac{p}{1+qz}$, and $y=\frac{pz}{1+qz}-a$. Were a workman to loan at interest his surplus y, or its equivalent $\frac{p}{1+qz}-a$, his total return would amount to $\frac{p}{1+qz}-az$. Now what rate of interest will make this amount the largest?

[1] *Der Isolirte Staat*, ii, p. 157.

The differential calculus yields for z the value $\frac{\sqrt{ap}-a}{ap}$. If we substitute this value of z in the equation $a+y=\frac{p}{1+qz}$, we have $a+y=\frac{p}{1+\frac{\sqrt{ap}-a}{aq}}=\frac{ap}{a+\sqrt{ap}-a}=\sqrt{ap}$. Hence it appears that when a laborer receives $\sqrt{ap}$ wages he receives the highest return on his surplus invested, and his interest coincides with that of the "capital producing laborers" when wages are at that figure.[1]

The critics of von Thünen may be roughly divided into two classes. First, those who deny the validity of the formula because of the unreality of the assumptions upon which it is based. Secondly, those who impeach the consistency of his mathematical reasoning. The second class is more worthy of attention, because a mathematical criticism requires a profounder study and clearer understanding of the author.

Roscher thinks that we cannot place so high a value upon the law as von Thünen does, for it could hold only where the severe struggle between capital and labor does not exist. In young agricultural colonies, where fruitful soil exists in superfluity, where every laborer can save a surplus, where there are no capitalists in the narrow sense, and all the laborers are nearly alike, and, furthermore, colonies where perhaps no industry exists that requires large capital or superior labor, there a wage of $\sqrt{ap}$ might be natural.[2] Schäffle takes a similar position when he says that the law is valid only for a hypothetical economy. It presupposes an unchanging technique, a mere replacement of the number of laborers, a constant price for grain, and other fictions which suppose variable amounts for constant. Especially does he regard the hypothe-

[1] *Der Isolirte Staat*, ii, p. 160.

[2] *Geschichte der Nationalökonomik in Deutschland*, p. 896.

sis of a constant number of laborers as in reality no basis for natural wages.[1] Likewise Lehr objects that in the formula the number of laborers who compete with each other and press down wages plays no part. But (p) the product will be affected by the number of laborers. With a growing population the amount of land not yet occupied becomes continually smaller and less productive. Under a given condition of technique, the transference to more intensive operations yields to the last laborer less and less. The more p approaches a in amount, the more does the formula lose its significance. If $p = a$, then the laborer can lay up nothing.

Objections as given above are shared by many other writers, as Leymarie, Mangoldt and Mithoff. Dr. Joh. von Komorzinski[2] has more recently and in greater detail pointed out one of von Thünen's limited assumptions which is worth noting by itself. Von Thünen had argued that it was for the interest of the laborer that his wages should be at such a point that the interest upon the investment of his surplus be as high as possible. This Komorzinski clearly points out would not be true for all laborers. The laborer has two sources of income: wages, and interest on savings. He desires that with a given effort the total income be as large as possible. The relative importance to the laborer of wages and interest on savings depends upon the quantitative relation which each has to the whole income. A laborer who is just beginning to save desires that his wage be as high as possible. The rate of interest upon his small investment is a relatively unimportant matter to him; while the laborer who has saved much during a long period may regard the amount of his wage as a matter of comparative indifference. His chief source of income being interest upon invested surplus, he is led to desire a maximum rate. If

[1] *Das Gesellschaftliche System der Menschlichen Wirthschaft*, 1873, p. 440.

[2] *Zeitschrift ür Volkswirthschaft, Socialpolitik und Verwaltung*, B. iii, Heft i, p. 27–62.

von Thünen's argument is to be valid, laborers must have saved an equal length of time and an equal amount.

These objections are for the most part only repetitions of von Thünen's stated assumptions, and we cannot suppose that he is taken unawares. Ricardo assumes for the economic world at large conditions which were familiar to him on the stock exchange, and upon these he developed principles of rent that might have been more accurately developed if he had been more familiar with farm economy. Subsequent thinkers have had to make the necessary corrections. Ricardo's assumptions were not so violent as to belie his observations, for he really thought his assumptions, in general, were true. This cannot be said of von Thünen. He did not attempt to develop principles of banking investment based upon farming experience. Had Ricardo written on the exchange he would have traversed paths familiar to him. When von Thünen wrote on farming he wrote accurately. He was a practical farmer, as well as a scientific thinker. The world of his assumptions and that of reality are too far removed from each other for us to suppose him ignorant of the radical difference between them. He is constantly drawing contrasts between reality and the isolated state. He has a different law of wages and of interest for each.

How shall we explain his confidence in a law based upon conditions so far removed from the real world and so lacking in completeness? Only on the assumption that he regarded present conditions as unnatural, and the wage of the present order as an unnatural wage. He said that the present regime was likely to result in the starvation and misery of the laboring classes. The present system must therefore lack equity. He professed to have investigated the relation of wages and interest from several standpoints, and to have found that, when wages were at $\sqrt{ap}$, they agreed with the nature of man, and of the physical world.[1] He regarded his formula as a foot-

[1] *Der Isolirte Staat*, ii, p. 206.

rule by which to judge whether a wage were at once natural and righteous. It was, therefore, to express a condition that in his opinion ought to exist, a goal which laborers ought to strive for, and one that employers and society should help labor to reach.

We cannot but admire the spirit of von Thünen, who, in mediating between the extremes of the adherents of the "iron law" and those of the socialists, endeavored to lay a scientific foundation for the elevation of mankind. That he does mediate is shown by an inspection of the formula. If p were equal to a, then, according to the equation, wages would equal the necessaries of life, and wages would absorb the entire product. But with von Thünen, p is always greater than $a + y$. Wages then would be above the necessaries, but below the total product. Most men regard this as just. Our admiration of his spirit, however, must not blind us to the faults of his work. A man may love his neighbor, and may give him a formula by the realization of which in life, he may be landed in a state of comfort and right economic relations with his fellows. But if that formula can be realized only in a state of society far removed in nature from the present, and if that state, in addition, is so primitive and simple as to preclude the social complexities of modern life, the author of the formula may not complain if he is rejected as an unsafe and impractical social guide. Such is the position to which von Thünen is reduced by this method of criticism.

The second method of criticism is quite as important in results, assuming the points well taken, because it discredits the mathematical reasoning by which the formula is evolved. The method of procedure is to show that von Thünen treated as constant or known some quantity which in reality is variable or unknown. Among the first to do this was Falck.[1]

[1] Falck, *Die Thünensche Lehre vom Bildungsgesetz des Zinfusses und vom naturgemässen Arbeitslohn.*

He says "the formula $\frac{[p-(a+y)]y}{q(a+y)}$ was obtained from the formula $\frac{n[p-(a+y)]}{\frac{nq(a+y)}{y}}$. The numerator denotes the rent from the farm, the denominator the number of those among whom the rent is divided. But is the y of the denominator really equivalent to the y of the numerator? The y of the numerator denotes the surplus that is paid to the laborer at this particular time; but the y of the denominator denotes the surplus of wages that existed before the laying out of the farm. Only by placing the two y's equal to each other has it been possible for the rent (or interest) to obtain a maximum value at a definite rate of wages."[1] This would be a just criticism if it were conceived that von Thünen was dealing with two widely different economic regimes at the same time. But a sympathetic study of von Thünen makes it fairly clear that he regarded the economic conditions under which both Group I and II worked as identical. He assumed that natural wages already existed in the isolated state; and as a means of discovering the mathematical expression for such wages, he supposed that a number of laborers, to whom it is a matter of indifference whether they labor for wages or cultivate a marginal farm on their own account, combined to lay out a farm.[2] If the social arrangements are the same in both cases; if the society is stationary, as the isolated state was conceived to be; if men were equal in skill and the standards of life were the same among them all, then the necessaries or life subtracted from an equal wage would have equal surplus, and the y's would be equal. Thus Falck's objection falls to the ground.

Komorzynski in the article referred to above also attacks

[1] Quoted by H. L. Moore in his *Von Thünen's Theory of Natural Wages.* See *Quarterly Journal of Economics*, v. 9, p. 389.

[2] *Q. J. of Econ.*, v. 9, p. 391.

the formula, but in a somewhat different way. He inquires whether a general relation between the rate of interest z and wage surplus y exists which finds its proper expression in $z = \frac{p-(a+y)}{q(a+y)}$. He defines p as the exchange value of the product after the deduction of all outlays except wages and interest on capital. $q(a+y)$ expresses the value of the capital invested. $q =$ the number of year's wages which equals the value of the capital. The question now relates to the propriety of treating p as constant, and of valuing capital in the manner indicated. That p should not be treated as a constant must be evident, says Komorzynski, from the fact that p is a different quantity in every different process of production. Moreover, it is straining matters to suppose p the same when great changes may occur in wages and interest. Likewise the value of the capital, a complex of goods, is treated as constant, although the formula for wages, a changeable factor, is used to express its value. It is difficult to regard capital as having a static value when it is itself a dynamic entity. The goods of capital become in turn products, and other goods take their place, yet the value is conceived as the same. Products of one process find application as capital in some other production process, in all of which cases von Thünen conceives the value of capital as dependent upon the rate of wages. Von Thünen does not seem to have applied a consistent theory of price determination. It follows that, if p and $q(a+y)$ vary by no known law with every different process of production, $z = \frac{p-(a+y)}{q(a+y)}$ cannot express a constant relation between interest and surplus in all industries. It is unsuited to express a general relation, however well it may represent the relation between wages and interest in specific industries.

Komorzynski errs in two particulars: first, in not remembering the static conditions of the isolated state; secondly, in disregarding the author's definition of p. Von Thünen nowhere has p represent value. If he speaks of mining, p stands for so many pounds of silver; if of agriculture, then so many bushels of rye. It will be seen that this error vitiates the argument of the example upon which he relies to prove his position. He says, "If the rate of interest is 5 per cent. and the rate of wages 400 florins, then, in three different forms of production, these equations may exist:

"I. $\frac{5}{100} = \frac{2500 - 400}{105 \times 400}$, where $p = 2{,}500$ and $q = 105$.

"II. $\frac{5}{100} = \frac{1200 - 400}{40 \times 400}$, where $p = 1{,}200$ and $q = 40$.

"III. $\frac{5}{100} = \frac{460 - 400}{3 \times 400}$, where $p = 460$ and $q = 3$.

"But if $(a + y)$ should rise from 400 to 450 florins, then the following unequal rates of interest would result:

"I. $\frac{4.33}{100} = \frac{2500 - 450}{105 \times 450}$.

"II. $\frac{4.16}{100} = \frac{1200 - 450}{40 \times 450}$.

"III. $\frac{.741}{100} = \frac{460 - 450}{3 \times 450}$."[1]

If p represents not value but product in kind, there is no necessity of assuming that p remains constant when the rate of wages changes. Why may not p change in quantity so that the value of the product may so adjust itself as to counteract the disturbance of a change in wages? In which case the rate of interest would remain the same.[2]

The only remaining criticism of von Thünen which will be noticed here is that by Professor H. L. Moore in the articles referred to above.[3] Says Moore, "Thünen's purpose in the

[1] Quoted by Moore, see *Quarterly J. of Econ.*, v. 9, p. 398.

[2] *Quarterly Journal of Economics*, v. 9, p. 399.

[3] *Ibid.*, April and July, 1895.

whole work is to find mathematical expressions for the natural rate of interest and the natural rate of wages. The method by which he does this is first to find a formula expressing the interdependence of wages and interest in the isolated state. The formula, $z = \frac{p-(a+y)}{q(a+y)}$, we shall call formula *A*. In this formula all the quantities are known except y and z. In order to find the values of y and z, he next attempts to find an independent expression for y or what is the same thing, since a is known, an independent expression for $(a+y)$; and by substituting for $(a+y)$ in formula *A* obtain the value of z. The formula which enables him to find the independent expression for $(a+y)$ is $\dfrac{n[p-(a+y)]}{\dfrac{nq(a+y)}{y}}$. In this formula, which we shall call formula *B*, all the quantities are assumed as known excepting y. But how did von Thünen obtain the quantity nq? He (von Thünen) says: Suppose 'the laying out of the farm required the year's labor of nq men .... Unquestionably in order to provide a new farm is needed not only labor, but also the use of capital; (but) according to § 13, we can reduce the co-operation of capital to terms of labor, and thus express the costs of laying out the farm entirely in terms of labor.' When we refer to § 13 to see how the reduction is to be performed, we find that it is done by means of the rate of interest. The fallacy in the argument is evident. Thünen's whole procedure is a mere begging of the question. His problem is to find the values of y and z in the formula *A*; and, to solve the problem, he undertakes to find an independent expression for $(a+y)$ by means of formula *B*, and by substituting for $(a+y)$ in formula *A* obtain the value of z. But, in order to get the quantity nq in formula *B*, he assumes that z is known. If, however, z is known, then, according to formula *A*, y is known. Thünen undertakes to find the value of the unknown quantities y and z; and, in attempting to solve the problem, he uses the very quantities that he wants to find as known quantities."[1] This expresses in the clearest possible manner Prof. Moore's position. It is a position which appears unassailable. I can discover no flaw in his argument; his study of von Thünen has evidently been thorough and candid. Of von Thünen's critics and commentators he seems to me to be the best informed on the author's fundamental ideas. He was the first adequately to grasp the true limitations of the isolated state; to note the true difference between the dynamic and static conditions of von Thünen's problem. A proper emphasis on the last mentioned point has enabled Prof. Moore successfully to defend von Thünen against those who have not adequately comprehended him. This same insight has enabled Prof. Moore to hit upon the real weakness of von Thünen's work, and to show that, after all the laborious work on the isolated state, the conclusion is worthless.

In two particulars, then, we find von Thünen's formula for wages unsatisfactory: First, assuming the conditions of the isolated state as admissible, the formula is not obtained by a proper method. Secondly, if the formula were properly obtained, it would be useless on account of the extreme limitations of the isolated state upon which the formula is based.

If the results based upon the isolated state may not be accepted, and it is found necessary to set aside that part of the discussion which relates to wages as of slight value, it will not be denied that there are some things of real interest in his treatment based upon the objective economic world. By many years von Thünen anticipitated a theory of prevailing wages[2] that was independently developed and made known to the world by Professor J. B. Clark—a theory which is quietly finding its way into the pages of economic works, and becoming a sort of common property with almost no knowledge or acknowledgment of its source. As will be seen, however, von Thünen found slight comfort in the theory for the future of the race.

[1] *Q. J. of E.*, v. 9, p. 405.

[2] *Der Isolirte Staat*, ii, p. 178–193.

He pointed out that an undertaker will not employ additional laborers unless they earn for him at least as much as he pays them. If the point of equivalence between return and wage-payment has been reached, then a rise of wages with a stationary value of product (*i. e.*, output of laborers) brings about a decrease of laborers employed, and, as a result, a decreased output. Further, an increase of value of product with stationary wages yields the opposite result, viz., additionally employed labor with an increased output. Since it lies in the interest of the undertaker to increase the number of his laborers so long as by their employment a net advantage accrues to him, the limit of that increase is reached when the output of the last laborer employed is entirely absorbed by his wages. The wages, then, of the last laborer employed must about equal his output. But these wages are normal for all laborers of like skill, because for like service unequal wages cannot be paid. Employing the term "marginal" for "last employed," we reach the following law: wages are determined by the product of marginal laborers.

Von Thünen did not discuss this doctrine in detail. Much was left to the easy acquiescence or imagination of the reader. For instance, one feels the lack of scientific explanation of the true significance of marginal employment. That von Thünen himself recognized the wide field of resort for the unemployed in the marginal uses of capital can scarcely be doubted, otherwise he could not have assigned so important an agency to it. That the theory attracted almost no attention among thinkers, who must be supposed to have read the work, may be attributed to its fragmentary treatment. As it stands in von Thünen's pages the theory is a digression. Von Thünen laid comparatively no emphasis upon the matter, because he was not primarily interested in the statement of the law of present wages. He was far more concerned with the discovery of a law of distribution, the realization of which should secure to the laboring class wages adequate to a reasonably high level of life. He was convinced that the present system did not do this. It was not enough for him if the wages received were equal to amount produced. More important was the inquiry: Are laborers secure from misery and want?

After stating the above theory of wages, he proceeds by means of the theory to correct some misapprehensions in regard to the labor problem. The socialists deny that one man, whatever his skill may be, should receive as much, or more, for an hour's work as another man receives for twelve hours. But, says von Thünen, it is idle to complain of an undertaker who pays his superintendent a superior reward. He pays it simply because the overseer's product at least equals his wages. The socialists' scheme of using labor time as a measure of wages is a dream. The misery of the laboring class cannot be laid to the fault of the "entrepreneurs," for they cannot pay more to labor than labor is worth to them. If some one objects that the earlier employed laborers produce more than they receive, and that thus the conductor of industry has a surplus at his disposal for higher payments which, if he withholds, makes him responsible for the laborers' lot, it is to be said that such an objection shows a confusion of moral and business principles. If one undertaker alone did what is here suggested he would be driven out of business by his competitors; and, if a nation did this, it would suffer by foreign competition. It may be laid down as an absolute principle that no laborers should be employed whose output does not cover the cost of their employment, otherwise the wealth of society, which ought to be increased by the labor force of a nation, would be by it diminished. No, the misery of the laboring class may not be remedied by an appeal to the sense of duty of the rich, but must be met in some other way.

Von Thünen proceeds to show by means of this law of wages that under the present system the fate of the laboring class may be a melancholy one. There seems to be no escape from the main conclusions of the theory. If we suppose wages to increase, without a decrease in the number of laborers, the last laborers employed do not earn their wages. Employers will then discharge men till the last one retained earns what is paid to him. Thereby many laborers are made idle, and rather than starve they will be willing to work for the old rate. Hence under these circumstances no rise of wages can occur. If, on the other hand, the laboring population should increase, while capital and land remain constant in amount, then the new laborers can find no employment at the present rates. This is plain from the fact that, since this wage already absorbs the entire product of the marginal laborers and every additionally employed laborer produces less than the one previously employed, the hiring of the new laborers at the present rate involves a loss to the undertaker. It follows that the new laborers can find employment only at a lower rate. If additional population makes necessary the employment of labor upon less and less productive objects, wages must continue to fall till the limit of subsistence is reached. The increase of population under these circumstances, bringing its attendant evils, seems, however, to von Thünen a certainty. But the evil, he thinks, will not fall upon all indiscriminately. He holds to the doctrine of the salvation and survival of the fittest. By constitution men differ in soundness and skill. By reason of life's changes men's industrial fitness differs with age. Hence if there is a surplus of population, only the healthy, the most skillful, the most efficient and those in the prime of life will be retained. The old, the decrepit, the weak, the inefficient will be industrially left behind. We may thus approach conditions in which the only relief from actual suffering is an appeal to charity funds. Reckless increase of population is an evil from which even good harvests may not rescue us. Von Thünen is haunted by the suggestion that prosperity (economically) gives well-being, well-being over-population, and over-population misery; and he asks whether there is no escape from this vicious circle. Has Providence designed that as the earth becomes inhabited, the future should become darkened by the vision of increasing misery? He thinks there must be an escape. Providence is not so cruel; but clearly to define the conditions whose fulfilment will ensure happiness to men, is a problem with which he cannot attempt to deal.

CHAPTER V

THE SOCIALISTS

WHAT is often called the pessimistic side of Ricardo's economic ideas, viz., the side which rests wages upon some necessary demand on the part of laborers, reached its highest development in the socialistic view of wages. Marx,[1] like Von Thünen, was dissatisfied with a simple appeal to supply and demand as an explanation of wages. According to him it explains nothing but wage changes. "The price of labor at the moment when supply and demand are in equilibrium is its natural price determined independently of the relation of supply and demand, and how this price is determined is the question at issue.[2] His treatment of wages is a unit with the treatment of the value of commodities. "That which determines the magnitude of the value of any article is the amount of labor socially necessary for its production."[3] The value of a commodity being determined initially by conditions of production, it is put into the course of trade or circulation in order to realize upon it, during the process of exchange, a surplus value. Commodity is exchanged for money, and money for commodity, so that with each transaction an increase of value or surplus is exacted. If it were otherwise, the exchange would not take place. A similar process, says Marx, occurs with respect to labor. To make this point clear, a distinction is made between labor-power and labor. By labor-power, or capacity for labor, is to be understood the aggregate of those mental and physical capabilities existing in the human being

[1] The references to *Capital* are to Sonnenschein's edition.

[2] *Capital*, p 548.

[3] *Ibid.*, p. 6.

which are exercised whenever there is produced a use value of any description.[1] Labor is labor-power in use.[2] A laborer is labor-power in action. The value of the two may be, and usually is, quite different. The value of labor-power is the price of labor on the market, or wages. The value of labor is the value of labor-power when it is embodied in a product; and that value must be greater than the former, as a rule, or the capitalists would not deal in labor. At one point in the discussion, Marx sees that the price of labor-power will be fixed by the bargaining powers of each party to the contract. He also says that the minimum limit of the price of labor-power is determined by the value of the commodities for consumption, which are required to renew labor energy and to renew the supply of laborers from fresh generations.[3] But in his further treatment he assumes that wages will not be much above this lowest limit. He does say that if it falls *to* this minimum it falls *below* its real value, for then it would exist in a crippled state. "The value of every commodity is determined by the labor time required to turn it out so as to be of normal value."[4]

The method of converting the value of labor-power into the value of labor and thus securing a surplus value, is the kernel of Marx' severe indictment against capitalistic production. Assuming that the product of six hours of labor almost covers the cost of the maintenance of labor, or wages, the capitalist class is guilty of wrongful appropriation of all values created in the remaining hours of the working day. This analysis of the industrial situation has considerable enforcement in Marx' historical account of movements to secure a shorter legal working day. Such movements have usually encountered the united opposition of the employing class. The inference is easy on a superficial view; it is because employers dread a curtailment of a surplus which they

[1] *Capital*, p. 145.

[2] *Ibid.*, p. 156.

[3] *Ibid.*, p. 152.

[4] *Ibid.*, p. 152.

have marked as their own. Marx' accumulated mass of evidence from the English Blue Books as to the barbarously long hours of labor of men, women and children, exacted in the early history of English manufacture, constitutes some of the most tragic chapters of history. His account is admirably calculated to enlist a lively sympathy for the innocent and almost helpless class of wage earners, and at the same time calls forth deep resentment against the powerful capitalists whom we are led to regard as heartless and rapacious to the last degree. The real point made here by Marx is that, as machinery has increased the efficiency of labor to the extent of enabling a worker to accomplish as much, say, in four hours as could formerly be done in ten, the hours of labor in a day have not been reduced in proportion.

It must not be lost sight of, however, that hours of labor have been materially shortened as society has become adjusted to machine and factory conditions of production. Where the factory system has developed most completely the hours are not so long as to excite pity. The condition of things in this respect under the domestic system, and in the early factory period, as well as those where older forms of production still survive, is far less favorable than in the fully developed factory system. In the second place, physical productivity of capital may not necessarily be value productivity. Under modern conditions laborers cannot, and ordinarily would not, desire to be paid in the commodities of their own making. They prefer payment in a universally acceptable commodity representing some proportionate value of their product. The working man is interested in the value of his total product, not in the number of pieces turned out. The figures commonly employed to show the enormous increase of productive power by the use of capital nearly always fix the attention upon the physical facts of the case, and the result is sufficiently startling. But if comparison were made only between the values of the product with and without machinery, a different impression would result, especially if account were taken of all the labor involved in the production of the capital. Those who read the earlier portions of Capital and not the later are apt to get erroneous notions of the amount of exploitation of laborers which exists according to socialistic conceptions. If six hours of labor are sufficient to support the worker, but the employer forces him to add four or six hours more to each day's labor for the employer's special benefit, an injustice is apparent. But if from the product of the additional hours, all capital which makes possible this large production for the laborer, must be replaced, and all losses incident to capitalistic risk must be met, the amount remaining over as a true surplus value on *a priori* grounds may not appear great. Marx does not ignore replacement of capital. "Whatever the form of the process of production in a society, it must be a continuous process, must continue to go periodically through the same phases." "When viewed, therefore, as a connected whole, and as flowing on with incessant renewal, every social process of production is, at the same time, a process of reproduction."[1] The very condition of production with the aid of capital, whether the economic organization be the so-called "capitalistic" or socialistic, requires that a large share of the annual income or social dividend be reconverted into means of production, or in other words, that it be devoted to the service of replacement of capital whose energies have been transmitted into products of a lower degree, to use Menger's conception. Marx has devoted much space to show the process of the flow of products and the conversion of a part of this flow into capital. And there is much in that part of his work which will repay diligent study.

However, Marx regards even the replacement of capital to be as much an exploitation as is the personal consumption of the capitalist. If we suppose that a capitalist has made an investment of a certain sum, and yearly devotes enough of the

[1] *Capital*, 1887, p. 577-8.

product to replace the yearly wear of the capital, and consumes the rest, it will be but a few years when he will have consumed a value equal to his capital. Now, the capitalist thinks that he has consumed the product of unpaid labor, says Marx, and that he has kept his capital intact. But that is not Marx' interpretation. In fact, the capitalist has consumed his own capital, which he may have himself produced, but has appropriated surplus value without payment to the amount of his original capital. Thus replacement is an exploitation.[1]

Of special interest is Marx' conception of the relation between wages and product, as well as between wages and capital. This relation is first indicated by an illustration.[2] A peasant, who is liable to do compulsory service for his lord, works three days for himself and three on the lord's domain. Under these circumstances the peasant reproduces his own labor fund. If the lord appropriates to himself the land and other means of production of this peasant, the latter will be obliged thenceforth to sell his labor-power to the lord. Under these circumstances, he continues to work three days for himself, the time necessary to obtain his necessaries, and three days for his lord. "As before, he will use up the means of production, as means of production, and transfer their value to the product. In the same way, a definite portion of the product will be devoted to reproduction [replacement]. But from the moment that the forced labor is changed into wage-labor, from that moment the labor-fund, which the peasant himself continues as before to produce and reproduce, takes the form of a capital advanced in the form of wages by the lord."

The economists of Marx' day regarded wages as advanced from capital, but Marx regards wages as paid from current product. He says that it is only here and there on the face of the earth that what laborers receive as wages is not what laborers have already themselves produced.[3] He complained of classical

[1] *Capital*, p. 582. [2] *Ibid.*, p. 580–1. [3] *Ibid.*, p. 581.

economy, that it always loved to conceive social capital as a fixed magnitude of a fixed degree of efficiency.[1]

As will be seen in the subsequent treatment, Marx regards the capital of a country as constantly changing in quantity, and in the relative proportions of its elements. Upon these two facts—accumulation of capital and the change in the constituents of capital—rests the fate of the working classes. As a first step in the argument, we must make clear what Marx meant by the terms constant and variable capital. In the processes of production, he desired to place in clear light the precise part which labor performed, as well as that of capital. It is a common observation that, under ordinary circumstances, values in means of production are perpetuated in their products. Of this there may be more than one explanation. One commonly entertained is that capital possesses the capacity in itself of erecting new values which take the place of those values dissipated while capital is performing its industrial functions. This view Marx rejects. Another explanation is that capital has no such capacity, but is a dead, inanimate, passive complex of things upon which labor operates. Capital can, therefore, create no values of any sort.[2] But human labor possesses the capacity to transfer values from capital, in which values already exist, to products. And this labor does unconsciously and inevitably while it is performing another function as well. It is a common observation of economic life that products possess greater value than is to be found in their means of production. The true explanation is, according to Marx, that while labor is transferring old value, it is also creating new value. Thus labor performs a double function in the same act. In the process of production itself, or that part of the process which is represented in the transferring of value, no quantitative change in value occurs. That part of capital which is represented by means of production, by the raw material, auxiliary

[1] *Capital*, p. 622. [2] *Ibid.*, p. 383.

material, and the instruments of labor, is called constant capital. On the other hand, that part of capital represented by labor-power does in the process of production undergo an alteration of value. "It both reproduces the equivalent of its own value, and also reproduces an excess, a surplus-value, which may itself vary; may be more or less according to circumstances. This part of capital is being continually transformed from a constant to a variable magnitude, and is called variable capital."[1]

Marx opposes the idea of Adam Smith and Ricardo, that capital in its ultimate analysis may be resolved into advances to labor. All surplus value is divided into means of production, and the direct support of laborers. It is illogical, he declares, to admit, as Adam Smith did, that in the case of the individual capitalist, all capital does take these two directions, and then deny it for the capital of society.[2]

Marx does not minimize the importance of capital as a productive agent. He shrinks from conceiving it as possessing power, preferring to regard capital as loaded with value transferable by labor. Although he is usually an unsparing critic of the capitalist class, at times he is forced to give capitalists credit for the social service of having forced the human race to produce and develop its powers. Without the capitalist, society might not have created the material conditions which alone can form the real basis of a high form of society, and in which the full development of every individual forms the ruling principle.[3] But in performing this service, the capitalist has exalted the principle of saving. Accumulation has come to be the law and the prophets. In Marx's view, at the bottom of all accumulation is the propensity and power to withhold from labor a part of its just share of social product. But capitalists are charged with having sometimes forced conditions which result in adding to their profits at the expense of laborers' necessary support. Wages are forcibly reduced below the value of labor power.

[1] *Capital*, p. 191–2. [2] *Ibid.*, p. 601. [3] *Ibid.*, p. 603.

A second factor in accumulation is relief from the necessity of furnishing capital in proportion to labor employed. Any given capital is made sufficient by requiring longer hours in factories, by day and night shifts in extractive industries, and by the reliance upon nature in agriculture as an immediate source of greater accumulation. The general result is that "by incorporation with land and labor, capital acquires a power of expansion that permits it to expand its accumulation beyond the apparent limits of its own magnitude.[1]

But the most important factor in accumulation is the productivity of social labor. All nature works in the interest of the capitalist. While machines are wearing out, and having their value transferred to products, science and technology are making their advances, the results of which are incorporated in the new machines without additional burden to the capitalist.[2] Then, too, labor's capacity to transfer value from capital to product in the very act of creating new value, is nature's gift, since it is done unconsciously and without merit on labor's part. Capital in this case is nature's beneficiary. The same fact becomes evident if we regard capital from another standpoint. As capital increases in quantity, the difference between fixed and circulating capital (to adopt an old classification, but excluding wages from circulating capital) increases. That is to say, the number and mass of those things which yield up their utilities but slowly, constantly increase in proportion to those whose utilities are transferred at once. Now, just so far, says Marx, as those things which lose their value piecemeal, are "wholly employed, but only partially consumed, they perform the same gratuitous service as natural forces, water, steam, air, etc. This gratuitous service of past-labor, when filled with a soul by living labor, increases with the advancing stages of accumulation."[3]

This general idea has further enforcement by a course of

[1] *Capital*, p. 616. [2] *Ibid.*, p. 617. [3] *Ibid.*, p. 620.

argument which is designed to show the influence of the growth of capital upon the fate of the laboring class, and which ends with a melancholy picture of the pauperism to which the laboring population of the world is inevitably tending by the very essence of the capitalistic mode of production.

Accumulation and consequent growth of capital yield the following results:

I. Diminution of the mass of employed labor in proportion to the mass of the means of production.

II. Accelerated diminution of variable as compared with constant capital.

III. Increase of surplus population more rapidly than the diminution of the variable part of capital.

Before taking these points in order, it is desirable to show a direct relation between accumulation and rate of wages. A rise in wages has one of two possible meanings, with reference to accumulation. Either it does not interfere with accumulation, in which case capital is in excess, not because labor power or labor population is diminished, but because, given excess of capital, exploitable labor-power is insufficient. It is not a case of stationary capital with a diminishing population, but one of increasing accumulation, and not enough laborers for capital to exploit with the highest advantage. Or, on the other hand, accumulation is reduced in consequence of the rise in the price of labor. In this case capital is insufficient, not because of increase of labor-power, but because, by a relative diminution of capital, there exists more labor-power than capital can exploit to the advantage of accumulation. The rate of accumulation is the independent variable; the rate of wages is the dependent one. The correlation between accumulation of capital and rate of wages is nothing else than the correlation between unpaid labor transformed into capital, and paid labor necessary to set the capital in motion. It is simply the relation between paid and unpaid labor of the same population. Wages rise whenever the quantity of unpaid labor increases so rapidly that its conversion into capital requires an extraordinary addition of paid labor, thus diminishing unpaid labor in proportion. But the movement of the rise of wages receives a check whenever this diminution touches a point at which surplus-population which nourishes capital, is no longer supplied in normal quantity, and accumulation lags.[1]

The first of the above propositions, viz.: that the mass of employed labor diminishes in proportion to the means of production,[2] is one very difficult to prove, and might be more difficult to deny. The fact that, in modern civilized countries, wealth increases more rapidly than population, creates a presumption that means of production increase faster than employed labor; but it is only a presumption. Observation, however, supports the view that as time proceeds, of the total capital employed, a larger proportion is devoted to purchase and maintenance of means of production. The diminishing proportion goes to pay for labor-power. It is desirable that this proposition should be put to some statistical test if it is to be used as a step in an argument. But Marx does not do that, but is satisfied with very general statements, such as that it is brought about by the compound ratio of impulses which the capitalistic mode of production and accelerated accumulation give one another,[3] or that it is due to the concentration of wealth, the domination of larger capitals, or the credit system.

In the second proposition, we have a more radical doctrine still. It is that variable capital diminishes at an accelerated rate as compared with constant capital.[4] Variable capital diminishes more rapidly than total capital increases. Increased accumulation and concentration of capital are regarded as the source of this new change in the composition of capital. We are not furnished with the proofs of the alleged fact, nor have we any convincing account of causes.

[1] *Capital*, 363-4.
[2] *Ibid.*, p. 636.
[3] *Ibid.*, p. 639.
[4] *Ibid.*, p. 643.

But the third proposition that surplus population increases more rapidly than the diminution of the variable part of capital,[1] is in greater need of demonstration than the others; Marx, however, does not supply it. If it were not maintained that variable capital was devoted to the support of the laboring population, that it is always distributed so meagrely as to supply mere encessaries, and that the laboring class had practically no other source of supply, it might not appear out of place to hold that population managed to exhibit signs of independence of the variable capital as the source of its food supply. It would be quite easy to believe that there existed no such strict correspondence between variable capital and population, as to prevent a slight relative increase or diminution of either. One might even admit for population a slower movement than for variable capital, the former lagging behind the latter. One might doubt whether population could increase in a constant ratio as variable capital diminished in the same ratio; but that population should actually increase faster than the variable capital diminishes, and that too not for short periods, but continually as a permanent movement, and furthermore, that this movement should be the natural fruit of accumulation, needs a logical statement of social and industrial sequences. But this is just what Marx does not give us. There are but hints as to the means by which the laboring population is made superfluous. Such are the magnitude of social capital, the degree of its increase, the extension of the scale of production, and of the mass of laborers set in motion, and the greater breadth and fullness of all sources of wealth.

These doctrines, supported by such reasonings, constitute the theoretical bases for Marx's law of wages. In this view, surplus population is a necessary product of accumulation. There is provided an industrial reserve army which it is for the interest of capital to have on hand for new enterprises, and as a general source of exploitation.

[1] *Capital*, p. 650.

Marx thinks that he has here hit upon the true explanation of general wages, which must be distinguished from any explanation of local wages. When the older economists explained a rise of wages as a consequence of increase of capital over population, and a fall of wages as a consequence of increase of population over capital, representing the population as in prosperous times increasing its numbers but in times of misery and want checking the increase, the explanation employs a local or temporary cause to account for a general or permanent movement. A working population tends to distribute itself over the entire field of production in obedience to the desire for the largest gain. Where capital is found in relative abundance, there capital tends to accumulate; and if the movement has given any locality a population relatively too large, wages fall and population tends to diminish. This, Marx says, is an accurate description of the relation between wages and the distribution of population over the different spheres of production. But it would be untrue to conclude that for all society when wages rise, population increases by reason of fewer deaths and more births per thousand; and that wages again fall as a result of a redundant population, because "before, in consequence of the rise of wages, any positive increase of the population really fit for work could occur, the time would have passed again and again."[1]

The other great exponents of German socialism were Rodbertus and Lassalle. Nothing but the briefest notice of their views can be given here. Rodbertus, like Marx, was a master mind, and it is noteworthy that, working quite apart, they came to much the same conclusions on many important points. Rodbertus, when he seriously compares modern laborers with slaves, states as strongly as possible the minimum support of labor as a determinant of wages. He regards the unlimited right to the fruit of one's own labor as the natural basis and essence of property right. He says that this principle is con-

[1] *Capital*, p. 651–3.

tinuously violated, in connection with the ownership of land and capital, by the present legal economic arrangements. That laborers have the fruit of their labor transferred to others is due to positive law and continual force.[1] Under slavery, the force, instead of being exercised by positive law, was exercised by the masters. They took the product, but gave the slave only as much as was necessary for the continuation of his labor. How is it under the present régime, when all the soil and all the capital have been made subject to private property? As under slavery, the product belongs not to the laborers, but to the lords of capital and land. As under slavery, laborers are comparatively happy if they secure from the product of their own labor such a part as is required for life's support; *i. e.*, for the continuation of their labor. If it is said that in place of slave possession we have free contract, it must be answered that the contract is only formally free. Hunger has taken the place of the whip. What was formerly called fodder is now called wages.[2]

This doctrine has become a fixed article in the theoretical economic creed of the German working men, largely through the agitation of Lassalle, who never lost an opportunity to enforce upon the Germans that their wages were down to the subsistence point, and that they were kept there, under present economic arrangements, by a law as inexorable as iron. As an authority for, and an expositor of, this law he appealed to Ricardo. If wages rise above the minimum more laborers are born into the world, and competition reduces their remuneration. If wages fall below the minimum labor population fails at the source, and again demand causes wages to rise.

It will not escape notice that on this point Marx and Lassalle were in opposition. Marx endeavored to strike deeper.

[1] *Das Kapital*, 1884, p. 214–5.

[2] *ZurBeleuchtung der Socialen Frage*, 1875, p. 33.

CHAPTER VII

SCHULZE-GAEVERNITZ

The reaction against the wages-fund theory, which was first expressed by Hermann and and carried on by Brentano and others, is issuing forth in a group of thinkers of which Schulze-Gaevernitz[1] is an important member. The earlier reactionists drew attention away from past accumulation in the hands of employers, as the true source of wages, to that of the consumers' income, which is devoted to the purchase of laborers' product. The latest development of wage theory in Germany holds the so-called residual theory, and points to the conclusion that in the evolution of centralized industry (Grossbetrieb) there falls to labor a continually more favorable share of the product. This view is summarized in three propositions:

(*a*) In respect to any given product the amount of reward which accrues to capital decreases, not only absolutely, but also relatively to labor.

(*b*) The amount which accrues to labor decreases absolutely with reference to a single product, but increases relatively.

(*c*) Within a defined product the amount falling to both capital and labor absolutely decreases with the development of centralized industry. The process is a cheapening of production in favor of the consumer.

(*d*) The increase of the national product makes possible for labor and capital an absolutely greater return, with the development of industry, but the share of capital relatively decreases, that of labor relatively increases.[2]

[1] See his *Der Grossbetrieb*, 1892.

[2] *Der Grossbetrieb*, p. 224.

It is held that in the earlier period of the modern industrial evolution the laboring classes still belonged psychologically to an earlier date. Their wages were more or less near to the so-called life minimum.[1] The great pioneers of industry, with disposable capital in their hands, had a double advantage. First, the new order of things with its high demand for capital gave its possessors a high bargaining power. Hence, interest was extrordinarily high. Secondly, the talent brought to bear in the new fields, being of a rare and special quality, deserved, and was able to obtain, great rewards. Both these forces, when united in the same individuals, as they usually were, in reference to the ownership and management of a given body of capital, gave them such advantage in the industrial order that the additional values created by the new organization fell easily into their hands. They may be said to have received the remainder after the usual costs were paid.

Since that initial period of capitalistic production to the present time a great change has occurred. Now capital has increased enormously and interest has been gradually falling for many years. And talents which were once so rare no longer enjoy the monopoly of old.[2] The characteristics of the early period were: high costs due to high interest and high prices, together with high profits due to the element of monopoly.[3] Our author justifies this régime on the grounds that in no other way could the great masses of capital, which were necessary for the successful conduct of business in the new order, be brought together, that the habits and traditions of an earlier time favored a comparatively inferior order of men in the industrial field, and therefore the large accumulations with high profits were necessary to win capable heads for industrial callings, and, furthermore, that these capable heads came to have political influence, and social development was pushed forward through the exercise of political power by

[1] Schulze-Gaevernitz, *Der Grossbetrieb*, p. 215.

[2] *Ibid.*, p. 218.

[3] *Ibid.*, p. 217.

the industrial element. In contrast with the characteristics of the opening period of modern industry, the present shows low costs due to low interest, and the substitution of more productive capital for labor; low prices with an advantage to the poor consumer, the laborer, whose real wages are thereby increased.[1] The struggle to lower costs is a leading motive and agency in centralized industrial development. A similar amount of capital, because of technical advance, produces more than it did fifty years ago. Interest and profit have not advanced, hence the increasing surplus must be going to labor.[2] Edward Atkinson, whom Schulze-Gaevernitz so often quotes, puts the case as follows: Wages are a remainder from the sale of the product. To ascertain the share of labor the following deductions must be made:

1. Replacement of capital used.
2. A sum equal to the average rate of profit on capital invested in the very safest securities, and enough in addition to cover risks.
3. Cost of materials.
4. Cost of the very best administration.
5. Taxation.

The remainder constitutes the wages of labor, whatever that remainder may be. Wages constitute all there is left, and under the inexorable law of competition of capital, the profits of capital are constantly tending to a minimum, while the rate and purchasing power of wages are constantly tending to a maximum.[3]

Let us now consider first the implication of these views, and then show their bases in theory. That laborers are absolutely better off now than they were in the early part of the century, there can be little doubt. But that the growing advantages of civilization are being secured more fully by the laboring classes relatively than by the other classes in society

[1] Schulze-Gaevernitz, *Der Grossbetrieb*, p. 219. [2] *Ibid.*

[3] Atkinson, *The Distribution of Products*, 1885, p. 70.

is by no means free from dispute. The question cannot be discussed properly apart from a consideration of the relative numbers in the social classes—those who live directly on the proceeds of capital, and those who depend upon the proceeds of manual labor. Marx' contention that there always exists a reserve army, although he may not have correctly traced a causal connection between the growth of such a reserve and accumulation, has enough truth in it to make the problem of the unemployed one of grave concern. Concentration of industry is certainly eliminating the small producer and small dealer and converting them into laborers. If the class laborers is constantly growing relatively larger, and the class capitalists is growing relatively smaller, the returns to capital, though relatively less per unit, could secure to the capitalist relatively more as a whole than the laborer progressively receives. The question of concentration of property is of great importance, because we desire to know not so much the progressive return to capital, as the progressive return to the capitalist.

Moreover, the annual wealth of a country is by no means measured by the products of manufacture, agriculture and trade—using these terms even in a wide sense; but must include the increase of the value of what from one standpoint may be called idle property. Such are city lots and other property that increase in value annually by mere situation and growth of population. These increased values accrue to persons as owners. Laborers have small share in these increments.

Further, it is not certain what these authors mean by capital. What is often called capital, and upon which the usual rate of interest is computed, is so often mere "water," and represents no real investment, but results from capitalization.

It is not, however, with the alleged fact of the relative gain of capital and labor in growing industry that we have in this essay primarily to do; but rather with the law of wages according to which the result is said to issue, viz., that wages are the residual share of the total national income to be distributed.

So far as known to the present writer, no German author has formulated in detail the grounds of this theory. But since the residual wage theory is the basis of Schulze-Gaevernitz' work, it is desirable to make some examination of it.

According to this theory, rent, interest, and profits are each governed in amount by independent laws, while wages remain as a residual share. The owners of land receive rent, the owners of capital receive interest, and the owners of undertakers' ability receive profits. Rent is fixed in amount by the Ricardian law. Interest is fixed by the law of supply and demand. Profit, the share of the undertaker as such, which hitherto had been confounded with the capitalist's share, has been of recent years differentiated as the peculiar reward for initiating and "captaining" industry, and has been assimilated to the law of rent for the use of land. Francis A. Walker, who called profits the rent of ability, has the credit of being the first clearly to expound in detail this theory of profits as well as the residual theory of wages. According to this view, profits may be stated in terms of the law of rent; profits are determined by the differences existing in the productiveness of different abilities or opportunities of employers engaged at the same time in supplying the same market.[1] Profits range from the return to the poorest undertaker, who receives ordinary wages and who is called the no-profit undertaker, to the return which is limited only by business ability.

All three shares are so determined that they can in no way interfere with the laborer's share. Thus runs the theory: "unless by their own neglect of their own interests, or through inequitable laws or social custom having the force of law, no other party can enter to make any claim on the product of industry, nor can any of the three parties already indicated carry away anything in excess of its normal share."[2] This state-

[1] Walker, *Political Economy*, 3d ed., 1888, p. 236; Marshall, *Principles of Economics*, 2d ed., 1891, Book vii., ch v., § 7.

[2] Walker, *Political Economy*, 1888, p. 251.

ment of the theory has been interpreted to mean that the laborer's share is wholly dependent upon the laborer's contribution to the total product.[1] This conclusion is not unnatural from an exclusive attention to particular parts of Walker's work,[2] and an endeavor to connect wages and laborer's contribution from the statement that "wages equal the whole product minus rent, interest and profits."[3] But attention to all that Walker has written on the question of distribution makes it reasonably clear that he did not intend to teach a strictly productivity theory. That is, he did not attempt to establish any identity between the sum of values received as wages, and the sum of values produced by labor in the productive co-operation. He attempted to show that, when all the factors are working under normal conditions, there is a process of carving out shares from the total product by all the productive factors except labor; that whatever may remain after the slicing process is complete goes to labor as its share. If, now, the total product is increased by the energy, economy or care of labor, assuming no change in the other factors, and assuming the absence of friction, that increase goes to labor. In other words, if laborers make the total larger, and no change occurs in the efficiency of the other factors, the enlargement of laborers' remainder equals the enlargement of the total. This is an identity between an increment of product attributable to labor and an increment accruing to wages. At most, by this theory, the productivity theory applies to an increment and does not extend to total wages. "So far as by their energy in work, their economy in the use of materials, or their care in dealing with the finished product, the value of that product is increased, that increase goes to them by the force of natural laws, provided only competition be full and free."[4]

[1] *Journal of Political Economy*, v. 2, pp. 77–87, especially pp. 81–2.

[2] See especially *Wages Question*, pp. 129, 130.

[3] Walker, *Political Economy*, 3d ed., 1888, p. 284.

[4] Walker, *Political Economy*, p. 251.

The Germans under consideration do not attempt to modify in any important particular the main feature of Walker's theory. Hence a consideration of this part of German theory calls for no extended criticism. Such would be a criticism, not of the German work, but of that of President Walker. It may be remarked, however, that an appreciation of the strength of this theory requires a careful consideration of wage conditions for short and for long periods of time. Attention to that difference might have saved some criticisms. Walker admits that for short periods his theory does not hold true.

When we have made all allowances, the theory fails to satisfy the mind completely. An efficient competition of capital is assumed, while the equally at times efficient competition of labor is minimized. Money wages are for the most part in the author's mind, and there is hence a lack of definiteness as to the true relation of capital to wages, and no determination of consumable goods as the source of real wages.

Bei Fragen zur Produktsicherheit wenden Sie sich bitte an:
If you have any questions regarding product safety,
please contact:

Walter de Gruyter GmbH
Genthiner Straße 13
10785 Berlin
productsafety@degruyterbrill.com